The Eighteen Lohan Skills

The Eighteen Lohan Skills

Traditional Shaolin Temple Kung Fu Training Methods

十八羅漢功

Translation and Commentary by Stuart Alve Olson

Edited by Patrick D. Gross

Valley Spirit Arts

Phoenix, Arizona

Library of Congress Control Number: 2015932276
ISBN-13: 978-1-5077-8420-4
ISBN-10: 1-5077-8420-1

Valley Spirit Arts, LLC
www.valleyspiritarts.com
contact@valleyspiritarts.com

Cover concept by Stuart Alve Olson.
Cover design by Patrick Gross.
Title page illustration by Alice McGee.

Bodhidharma (菩提達摩, Pu Ti Da Mo,
fifth or sixth century CE, popularly known as Damo)
is the attributed founder of the Shaolin Temple
martial art tradition and is said to have brought
Chan (Zen) Buddhism to China.

Shaolin Temple (少林寺, Shao Lin Si)

Illustrations and Texts

The text, graphics, and photographs in the first section come from the Chinese work *Lohan Gong* (羅漢功) by Wong Honfan (黃漢勛, Huang Hanxun in Mandarin), published by Yin Mei Book Company, Hong Kong, 1980 edition. The images in the second section come from a Chinese text also titled *Lohan Gong*. Reproduction by Martial Studies Publishing Company, Taipei, Taiwan, 2006. No author is listed and no credit is given to any illustrator. The text in the third section of the Buddhist Eighteen Lohan Figures comes from *Biographies of the Eighteen Lohan* (八羅漢傳記十, *Shi Ba Lohan Zhuan Ji*). Compiled and printed by Fragrant Hill Temple (香山寺, Xiang Shan Si), no author listed.

Since this book contains spiritual images and text, please avoid leaving the book on the floor or any place where it may be stepped on or damaged, and do not bring it into bathrooms or unclean places. A longstanding rule in Buddhism states that there is a heavy karma for denigrating the images of the Lohans, so view them with respect.

Contents

Introduction 1

Part One: Eighteen Lohan Exercises

Praise Explaining the Results of the Skills 17

First Exercise: Immortal's Hands in Salutation 18

Second Exercise: Tyrant King Lifts the Cauldron 27

Third Exercise: Planting Flowers to the Left and Right 38

Fourth Exercise: Twisting the Roots of an
    Old Withered Tree 55

Fifth Exercise: Yaksha Searches the Sea 67

Sixth Exercise: Push Open the Window
    to Let in the Light 78

Seventh Exercise: Wei T'o Hands Over the Pestle 88

Eighth Exercise: Old Buddhist Monk Enters Chan 97

Ninth Exercise: Iron Ox Ploughs the Earth 107

Tenth Exercise: Green Dragon Wags Its Tail 117

Eleventh Exercise: Left and Right Mount the Horse 128

Twelfth Exercise: The Swallow Sips Water 135

Thirteenth Exercise: Person Fleeing From a Tiger 148

Fourteenth Exercise: Chen Tuan's Great Reason 158

Fifteenth Exercise: Father and Son Requesting Rites 169

Sixteenth Exercise: A Carp Thrashing About 180

Seventeenth Exercise: Zhang Lao Offers a Robe 187

Eighteenth Exercise: Jar Hanging on a Golden Hook 198

Part Two: Shaolin Lohan Skills

First Exercise: Yaksha Searches the Sea 206

Second Exercise: Push Open the Window
   to Let in the Light 210

Third Exercise: Wei T'o Hands Over the Pestle 214

Fourth Exercise: Old Buddhist Monk Enters Chan 218

Fifth Exercise: Iron Ox Ploughs the Earth 222

Sixth Exercise: Green Dragon Wags Its Tail 226

Seventh Exercise: Left and Right Mount the Horse 230

Eighth Exercise: The Swallow Sips Water 232

Ninth Exercise: A Person Fleeing From a Tiger 236

Tenth Exercise: Chen Tuan's Great Reason 240

Eleventh Exercise: Father and Son Making
   Three Requests for Rites 244

Twelfth Exercise: A Carp Thrashing About 248

Thirteenth Exercise: Zhang Lao Offers a Robe 250

Fourteenth Exercise: A Jar Hanging on a Golden Hook 254

Fifteenth Exercise: Tyrant King Lifts the Cauldron 257

Sixteenth Exercise: Planting Flowers
   to the Left and Right 262

Seventeenth Exercise: Twisting the Roots
   of an Old Withered Tree 266

Part Three: Buddhist Eighteen Lohan Figures

Deer Sitting Lohan 274

Happy Lohan 276

Raised Bowl Lohan 278

Raised Pagoda Lohan 280

Meditating Lohan 282

Overseas Lohan 284

Elephant Riding Lohan 286

Laughing Lion Lohan 288

Open Heart Lohan 290

Raised Hand Lohan 292

Thinking Lohan 294

Ear Scratching Lohan 296

Calico Bag Lohan 298

Plantain Lohan 300

Long Eyebrow Lohan 302

Doorman Lohan 304

Taming Dragon Lohan 306

Taming Tiger Lohan 308

About the Translator 311

Introduction

The original purpose for translating this work was to provide source material for my Praying Mantis Kung Fu students, as the Eighteen Lohan Kungs are a critical and foundational set of exercises for the development of kung fu in both the traditional Shaolin Temple and Praying Mantis schools. Also, frequent references are made in the martial art world to these Eighteen Lohan Skills, yet no full translation or serious analysis of this work exists in English, which is surprising considering the importance of the work to the martial art community. Without question, these exercises are the source for almost all martial art systems, not only is this true in the application and function of the exercises, but in posture names as well.

In presenting these teachings I made exclusive use of the original Chinese text by Fan Xudong (范旭東) and the later publication by Master Wong Honfan. I have also included the original illustrations from Fan Xudong's work and the photographs of Master Wong Honfan performing the exercises as they appeared in his book *Lohan Gong*.

Through its yoga-like stretching aspects, the Eighteen Lohan Skills are not only a qigong practice (combining breathing with body movements), they also train martial applications, and promote internal alchemy skills because they stimulate and develop the internal energies (Three Treasures) of jing (body/essence), qi (breath/vitality), and shen (mind/spirit). The Eighteen Lohan Skills, then, are a complete system for health, longevity, and spiritual immortality that combine aspects of yoga, qigong, martial art, and internal alchemy into one.

This book contains three sections, including the instructions for Fan Xudong's Eighteen Lohan Exercises, the Shaolin Lohan Skills, and the description of the eighteen Buddhist Lohans. What's interesting is that there's really no historical connection between the Lohan Skills presented by Fan Xudong (Part One), the original boxing text from Shaolin (Part Two), and the Eighteen Lohan figures (Part Three), even though they all share the name of "Lohan." Although associations between these sections consistently appear in Chinese sources, no solid evidence of the connections exist, as too much appears to be just wild and convenient history. With that said, however, these three main sources on the Eighteen Lohans and their attributed exercises are presented in this work because together they provide a fuller picture of this art that uniquely encompasses qigong, yoga, martial art, internal alchemy, meditation, and philosophy.

The popular belief is that Bodhidharma created these eighteen exercises, but this is highly unlikely. The exercises themselves include more Daoist-type figures than Buddhist, and the names of the exercises are not correlated with the actual names of the Buddhist eighteen Lohans. So, why are these Eighteen Lohan Skills associated with the persons of the eighteen Lohans? To frame this unanswerable question, we must go back into Buddhist history to note the original set of four Lohans with whom Buddha entrusted as protectors of the teachings. This number increased over time to sixteen Lohans as seen in Japanese and Tibetan Buddhist temples, and finally in China, during the Tang dynasty, the number was completed with eighteen Lohans.

If we can't answer why the Lohans are associated with the exercises, then why bother including the descriptions of these eighteen Lohans (the actual persons) in this work? No other books, including Chinese ones, have done this.[1] The reason relates to my opinion, and of many other teachers, that the learning of kung fu should always be accompanied with a spiritual-philosophical counterpart. To just learn kung fu as a means of strengthening the body or to encourage martial art skills without paying equal attention to its spiritual-philosophical roots is insufficient for grasping the full art, and limits the benefits of the teachings. Shaolin Temple was not a martial art center purely for learning how to fight, it was more a spiritual community dedicated to the propagation of Buddhist ideals and Chan (Zen) meditation. Kung fu enabled the monks to endure the rigors of Chan meditation. So, studying the spiritual qualities and lives of these eighteen Lohans unquestionably improves one's views and actions in the use of kung fu.

In present times, kung fu attitudes are more motivated by arrogance, rather than humility; more based on brute force than actual skill; more based on the fear of not winning, and less on the higher attitude of understanding losing—or, as my teacher would say to admonish rambunctious students, "Big loss, big gain." Kung fu is more a matter of spiritual discipline than that of base yearnings to be tough. Always keep in mind, no matter how good your kung fu fighting skills are, someone else is always better. The point here is that it's better to aspire to the stage of a Lohan than it is to become a great fighter.

---

1   For an informative historical depiction of this development of the Lohans, see "The Eighteen Lohans of Chinese Buddhist Temples" by T. Watters in *The Journal of the Royal Asiatic Society,* 1898.04, pp. 329–347.

Ultimately, it takes more courage not to fight than to fight, and this is especially true of those with great fighting skills. Therefore, I feel it is important to elevate a kung fu student's sense of humility rather than encourage arrogance about fighting skills. For all the above reasons, I felt it necessary to include the section describing the eighteen Lohans, and I hope that readers and students will examine this section carefully. Also, even though we don't know why the exercises were associated with the Lohans, this connection does exist. It appears that in the ancient tradition of Shaolin each of the Eighteen Lohan skills were associated with an individual Lohan, but that association has obviously been lost or hidden, and so in the Tang dynasty, with the inclusion of the seventeenth and eighteenth Lohan figures, the exercises were made to reflect Chinese spiritual figures and ideas, rather than an Indian source. This is just my opinion, however, not historical fact.

Terms, History, and Important Persons

Lohan (羅漢) is the Chinese term for Arhat in Sanskrit. Originally the Chinese transliterated this term as *A-Luo-Han* (阿羅漢), but later simplified it to "Lohan." The Lohan are considered the personal disciples of the Buddha, sixteen are Indian in origin and the remaining two are obviously Chinese, *Taming Dragon* and *Taming Tiger.* These two are definitely Daoist figures as the Dragon and Tiger represent *qi* and *jing*[2] in the

---

2   *Qi* (氣) and *Jing* (精) represent the vital-life and sexual energies in a person. From "taming" or, as a Daoist would say, "regulating" them, the internal elixir and spirit (神, *Shen*) for immortality is accomplished. In Daoism, jing, qi, and shen are collectively called the "Three Treasures" (三寶, San Bao).

internal alchemy teachings of Daoism. The inclusion of these two Chinese Lohan appears to be an effort to merge the immortality teachings of Daoism into the Shaolin tradition. This seems probable because in the text of the Eighteen Lohan Skills there are more Daoist figures used in title names than Buddhist. Actually, only two Buddhist references are made: *An Old Buddhist Monk Enters Chan* and *Wei T'o Hands Over the Pestle*.[3]

The four enlightenment stages of Arhats are 1) *Stream-Enterer,* 2) *Once-Returner,* 3) *Non-Returner,* and 4) *Arhat (Fully Awakened One)*.[4] The *Stream-Enterer* is said to have opened the Dharma Eye; meaning, they can intuitively understand the teachings of the Buddha and follow the Eightfold Path. Within seven rebirths, Stream-Enterers will attain complete Arhatship. The *Once-Returner,* literally meaning "once arriving," has weakened all attachments of greed, anger, and delusion. The Once-Returner only returns to human form one more time as the name suggests, but may cultivate in one or more of the Buddha lands before returning to the human world. The *Non-Returner,* meaning "never arriving," is reborn in one of the Buddha lands to attain Nirvana. The *Arhat* (Lohan) means "fully awakened one" or "deathless one," and is actually a Buddha. The term "Buddha," however, is reserved solely

---

3   Wei T'o, a Buddhist Mahayana bodhisattva (enlightened being), is considered a protector of Buddhist monasteries and the teachings of the Buddha.

4   In Buddhist spiritual literature, a work titled *The Sutra in Forty-Two Sections* (四十二章經, *Si Shi Er Zhang Jing*) explains the Four Arhat stages. See *Sutra in Forty-Two Sections* by Tripitaka Master Hsuan Hua, Buddhist Text Translation Society.

for Siddhartha Gautama Buddha, especially in Theravada Buddhism—out of respect for the fact that he discovered the path of enlightenment and Nirvana all on his own, without teachers and scriptures to guide him.

The term "Arhat" translates as "beyond death" or "deathless," more precisely in the spiritual sense, and so has a similar meaning to the Daoist term and ideal of an "immortal."

Bodhidharma was the twenty-eighth patriarch of Buddhism in India and the first patriarch of the Chan (Zen) Sect in China. Because he was a prince from southern India, he was able to have audience with Emperor Wu of Liang (梁 武 帝, Liang Wu Di) in 527 CE. At this time Buddhism had already been introduced into China, but its main influence was more on a literary level than an actual spiritual or religious practice. Bodhidharma eventually ended up taking residence at Shaolin Temple on Mt. Song (嵩 山, Song Shan) in Henan province, specifically to meditate in a small cave. This is evidenced by the back wall of the cave being permanently bleached with the outline of his body, caused by his sitting for long periods each day with the sun at his back.

Buddhist lore relates that when Bodhidharma gave Hui Ke (慧 可), his successor and second patriarch of the Chan Buddhist

Sect, the *Lankatavara Sutra*[5] (楞伽經, *Lengqiejing),* he told him,
    I present and pass on to you this *Lakatavara Sutra* in
    four scrolls. This is the essential teaching of the mind-
    ground of the Thus Come One [Buddha], by which you
    may lead all sentient beings to the truth of the Buddha
    teachings [Dharma].

Bodhidharma taught Hui Ke the Chan meditation practices,
and possibly wrote the *Damo Chan Classic* (達摩禪經, *Damo
Chan Jing)* under his name while at Shaolin.

A prominent misconception about Bodhidharma is the
popular notion that Shaolin martial arts were first introduced by
him. This persistent claim of Bodhidharma first teaching Shaolin
monks the qigong exercises of the *Muscle Change Classic* (易筋
經, *Yi Jin Jing),* the meditation methods of the *Marrow Cleansing
Classic* (洗髓經, *Xi Sui Jing),*[6] and later teaching them the Five
Animal Kung Fu,[7] and Eighteen Lohan Skills is completely
erroneous. The martial art tradition at Shaolin Temple preceded
Bodhidarma's arrival to China by a few centuries. Obviously,

---

5   See *Lankatavara Sutra* by Red Pine. Also, *Lankavatara Sutra:
     A Mahayana Text* by D.T. Suzuki.

6   The *Yi Jin Jing* and *Xi Sui Jing* manuscripts were supposedly
     discovered in Bodhidharma's coffin along with one shoe. For a
     translation of the *Yi Jin Jing,* see *Muscle Change Classic* by Yang
     Jwingming.

7   *Five Animal Kung Fu* consists of the Tiger, Dragon, Snake,
     Leopard, and Crane Styles. See *Five Animals Kung* by Doc Wai
     Fong, Unique Publications.

Bodhidharma's name was simply borrowed and attached to those works to lend more weight and importance to the practices. There is also the problem that Bodhidharma stayed at Shaolin Temple to undergo a nine-year meditation and vow of silence vigil, not to teach kung fu. The reputation of Shaolin Temple on Mt. Song is probably one of the most influential and famous of all Chinese institutions, both as a main center for Chan Buddhism and kung fu—so with this fame comes many misconceptions about its history.

Buddhist lore implies that Bodhidharma stayed at Shaolin Temple until a successor of his new lineage of Chan Buddhism was found. The successor turned out to be Hui Ke, and he was a former high ranking military officer, who through dissatisfaction with the world left home to become a monk. Hui Ke certainly would have known martial art and so would have further promoted the practice of kung fu with the resident monks.

Praying Mantis Boxing (螳螂拳, Tang Lang Quan). In the mid 1500s a Daoist priest from Shandong province named Wang Lang (王朗) created a new style of kung fu,  calling it Praying Mantis Quan. The short story behind this claims that Wang Lang had gone to Shaolin Temple to test his martial art skills and was easily defeated by the Shaolin monks.

On his return to Shandong province, he happened to see a praying mantis fighting with a cicada, a fight which the praying mantis easily won despite its smaller size. Wang Lang studied the insect's techniques and so created a new system of kung fu.

After some time he returned to Shaolin Temple and defeated the best monks using his Praying Mantis techniques. He then accepted two Daoist priest disciples, Sheng Xiao (升霄) and Yu Zhou (宇宙) in Shandong province.

Sheng Xiao taught Li Sanjian (李三剪) who then taught Fan Xudong. Fan included the Eighteen Lohan Skills in his five-volume series on Shaolin teachings. He gave a copy of his work to Luo Guangyu, who in turn gave it to Huang Hanxun, who is responsible for having made these exercises available to the public at large.

Yu Zhou, in turn, taught Li Sanjian's brother, Li Erkou (李二苟), and from this lineage stream the famous Master Wei Xiaotang (衛笑堂) was taught Praying Mantis Quan, specifically 八步螳螂拳 (Ba Bu Tang Lang Quan).[8]

This lineage information is being mentioned not only because these teachers incorporated the Eighteen Lohan Skills into their styles, which almost all Praying Mantis Quan lineages did for that matter, but also because of Wei Xiaotang's connection to my teacher, Master T.T. Liang (梁東才, Liang Dongcai).

In the early 1900s Feng Huanyi (馮環義, 1879 to ?) was the teacher of Master Wei Xiaotang, whom my teacher befriended and learned from in Taiwan in the 1970s. Wei Xiaotang

---

8   Master Wei Xiaotang was the lineage holder of Eight-Step
     Praying Mantis Quan (八步拳, Ba Bu Quan).

prescribed to six of the Lohan exercises for the training of his students. The Eighteen Lohan Skills have, in essence, become part of almost all Praying Mantis Quan styles (especially that of Seven-Star Praying Mantis Quan, 七星螳螂拳, Qi Xing Tang Lang Quan), and it is the Praying Mantis system that appears to be keeping the tradition of the Eighteen Lohan Skills alive. Very little propagation of these skills, surprisingly, comes from the Shaolin Temple tradition.

Fan Xudong (范旭東, 1841 to 1925, or 1936). Fan, like all early Praying Mantis Kung Fu students, was from Shandong province and a student of Master Li Sanjian, a second generation disciple of the Wang Lang Praying Mantis lineage.[9]   Fan reportedly traveled to Shaolin Temple frequently and studied the history, practices, and lifestyles of the monks there. Later in his life he compiled a five-volume series titled *The True Transmission of Shaolin* (少林真傳, *Shao Lin Zhen Zhuan),* or as some translate it, *The Authentic Shaolin.* These five volumes contained a range of Shaolin teachings, such as on medicine, acupuncture, kung fu, meditation, and so on. Within the books, he presented the original Eighteen Lohan Skills, along with the original text and drawings of a Shaolin monk performing the exercises. Fan

---

9   Some traditions list Fan Xudong as a Praying Mantis Kung Fu disciple of Wang Rongsheng (王榮生), but in Master Wei Xiaotang's *Praying Mantis* book, Fan is listed as a disciple of Li Sanjian, and Wang Rongshen as Fan's disciple. This is only being brought up because it raises the question of why would Fan Xudong give Luo Guangyu copies of *The True Transmission of Shaolin* and not Wang Rongsheng?

Xudong reportedly hand copied all the material and placed it within his work.

Luo Guangyu (罗光玉, 1888 to 1944). As a disciple of Fan Xudong, Luo Guangyu received copies of Fan's five-volume handwritten works, and thus incorporated the Eighteen Lohan Skills into the Seven-Star Praying Mantis Kung Fu tradition. Luo Guangyu should actually be credited with the survival and propagation of the Eighteen Lohan Skills, as he reportedly was adamant about his students learning these exercises.

Huang Hanxun (黃漢勛, Wong Honfan in Cantonese, 1919 to 1973). A disciple of Luo Guangyu, Huang reproduced the Eighteen Lohan Skills section of Fan's book and added photos of himself performing the exercises (translated and presented herein). Huang wrote over forty books on Praying Mantis Kung Fu and has earned the moniker of "Mantis King."

The Eighteen Lohan Skills

Although the exercises in this book may seem to be a non-martial art, they definitely are practiced as kung fu self-defense methods. Many of the techniques used within Praying Mantis styles are found in the Eighteen Lohan Skills, as well as in every other martial art system. This is not a question of Wang Lang or any of his descendants transposing Eighteen Lohan Skills into a new style of kung fu. All Chinese martial art styles have similarities to each other, yet each have their own distinctions as well, and the Eighteen Lohan Skills were developed long before other more popularly known systems of martial art—and qigong practices as well.

Below is just a short list of available works relating to the Eighteen Lohan Exercises. There are many Chinese works on the subject of Lohan Kung Fu, and a few works in English. Also, a great deal of information appears on the Internet concerning the kung fu aspects of the Eighteen Lohans.

Chinese Books:

- *Shaolin Temple Lohan Boxing* (少林寺羅漢拳, *Shao Lin Si Luo Han Quan)*. Published by Mt. Song Shaolin Temple, 1980.

- *Shaolin Lohan Boxing* (少林羅漢拳, *Shao Lin Luo Han Quan)* by Feng Zi (風子). Published by Hong Kong Guang Ming Book Company, 1958.

- *Lohan Gong* (羅漢功). Reproduction by Martial Studies Publishing Company, Taipei, Taiwan, 2006. Shows the original Chinese text and images of the Lohan exercises. Thought to be the original Shaolin Temple version that Fan Xudong used for his rendering in *The True Transmission of Shaolin*.

- *The Eighteen Lohan Hands* (羅漢十八手, *Lohan Shi Ba Shou)* by Huang Junming. Yin Mei Book Company, Hong Kong, 1980. Reproduction edition. Shows the Eighteen Lohan Exercises in their more qigong fashion.

- *The Master's Gate of Mount Hu: Shaolin Lohan Boxing* (護山子門少林羅漢拳, *Hu Shan Zi Men Shaolin Lohan Quan)* by Xia Tian. Yin Mei Book Company, Hong Kong, 1980. Reproduction edition. Shows a martial art form of the Eighteen Lohan Exercises.

- *Northern Praying Mantis Eighteen Venerables Boxing*
  (北螳螂十八叟拳, *Bei Tang Lang Shi Ba Sou Quan).*
  Yin Mei Book Company, Hong Kong, 1982. Shows
  a form from the Seven-Star Praying Mantis system.
  The term "Eighteen Venerables" is a reference to the
  Eighteen Lohan figures as presented in the third section
  of this work.

English Books:
- *Huang Han Xun: Luohan Gong, Shaolin Internal Training
  Set.* Translated by Wang Ke Se and Leonid Serbin.
  Published by Shaolin Kung Fu Online Library, 2006.
  This is a PDF version of the book, but the translation
  is incomplete.

- *The Eighteen Arhat Methods of Shaolin Kungfu* by Cai
  Longyun. Translated by Huang Long. Hai Feng
  Publishing Company, Hong Kong, 1986. This book
  shows the martial applications of the Eighteen Lohan
  techniques.

- *Northern Praying Mantis* by Stuart Alve Olson. Blue
  Snake Books, Berkeley, California. Includes a brief
  history of Praying Mantis Quan and shows the six Lohan
  exercises that Master Wei Xiaotang used in his teachings.

Conclusion

I am certain this work will inspire many questions, as it did for
me while compiling it. There's something very intriguing about
the subject of the Lohans, both in the exercises and the persons
with whom they are associated. Being a Taijiquan and Praying

Mantis Quan practicer I can clearly see the influences of these Lohan exercises on both arts. Likewise, having been a Buddhist cultivator for many years, I can also see the fusion of Hinayana and Mahayana Buddhism, along with Daoism, taking place in these texts.

I truly wish there were clear answers about the origins of these exercises and texts, but this pales in comparison to the fact that they are incredible teachings, useful to anyone who partakes in the serious cultivation of them. In this regard, I hope readers will find many golden nuggets of information, so no matter the style of martial art practiced they will benefit from reading this work.

—Stuart Alve Olson

Part One
Eighteen Lohan Exercises

少林真傳

古育黎范旭東氏錄

The True Transmission of Shaolin
Ancient Yu Li, "The Sun Rises in the East" Family Record

[Photo of Master Huang Hanxun]

Praise Explaining the Results of the Skills

It is important to complete these active skills[10] for cultivating nourishment.

Study diligently the practices of the pushing, striking, and palming.

Cease having a heart like a monkey and a mind like a horse.

Do the initial work of making lively the sinews, bones, spirit, and qi.

Spare no effort in ridding yourself of bad influences from others.

Initially be fixed about distinguishing the yin and yang of Wu and Zi.[11]

Completely transport and accumulate the energy of the entire body.

These [skills] are profound and mysterious, limitless, measureless, and constant.

---

10 *Active Skills* (行功, Xing Gong) is literally defined as "working actively," yet is normally only used in the context of the Nourishing Arts. Its meaning has overtones of "practicing," "exercising," and even "yoga." Xing Gong reflects more the idea of "moving meditation," whereas seated meditation is normally referred to as *Jing Gong* (靜功) "Stillness Skills."

11 *Wu*, hour of the Horse (11:00 a.m. to 1:00 p.m.) and *Zi*, hour of the Rat (11:00 p.m. to 1:00 a.m.).

First Exercise

Immortal's Hands in Salutation

仙 人 拱 手

Xian Ren Gong Shou

Original Text

Creation and destruction are healing and transforming.

Fix the breathing so each inhalation and exhalation can induce the qi, and complete the spirit with an empty mind.

Fill the abdomen with qi and blood so they can be nourished, and produce saliva to fill the abdomen.

Once this is accomplished, the qi in the abdomen will become abundant and then it can respond to the mind.

Raise the qi through the nostrils and retain in your mind a natural listening.

Accumulate the strength of the qi with these active skills and the result will be strength and health.

First Movement

The Two Hands Extend Straight Out to Push
The Two Feet Are Placed On Line With Each Other
雙直推兩脚並立

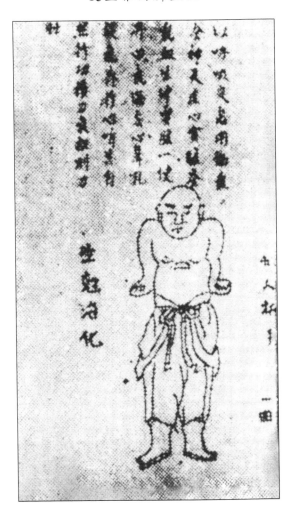

Practice Method

Stand with the feet placed together. The hands are firmly grasped into fists and pulled in to the fullest extent and held there [along the ribs and sides of the body—called a "Four Levels Posture"].[12] The eyes are fixed gazing directly forward. Simply allow the breathing to be natural.

12 Text in brackets are translator's comments. *Four Levels Posture* is so named because the shoulders, elbows, fists, and feet are all maintained in level positions.

Second Movement
Turn Over the Hands to Raise the Cauldron
Relying on the One-Breath
翻手舉鼎賴一口氣

Practice Method

From the first position both feet remain unmoved, but the two fists along the sides of the waist are moved directly forwards and out. As the fists move outward, exhale the qi.

When the fists are extended fully outward, turn them over so they appear to be clutching [hold the breath as they are turned over]. Continue to grasp the fists and slowly draw them back to the sides of the waist again [inhaling as they are drawn back].

Repeat these movements eight times and pause.[13]

---

13 When the instructions say to "pause," this indicates moments for holding the breath to accumulate the qi.

Third Movement
Bend the Knees to Lower the Waist
Completing the Prostrations to Conduct the Rites
曲膝下腰伏底放禮

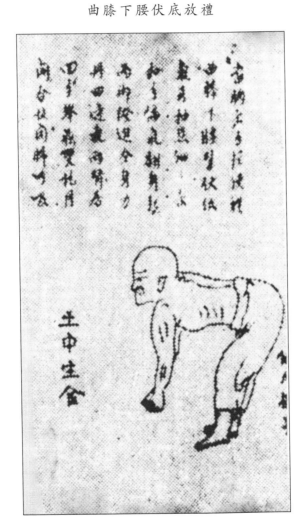

Practice Method

From the previous position, raise both clenched fists quickly upwards from the sides of the waist, inhaling the qi while doing so.

Next, turn the palms over while moving them downwards until the fists touch the ground [or tops of the feet], and exhale the qi while doing so.

Connect these upward and downward movements so to repeat them eight times.

Fourth Movement
Look Upwards to Face Heaven
Hollow the Waist to Strengthen the Stomach
仰面朝天凹腰䐃肚

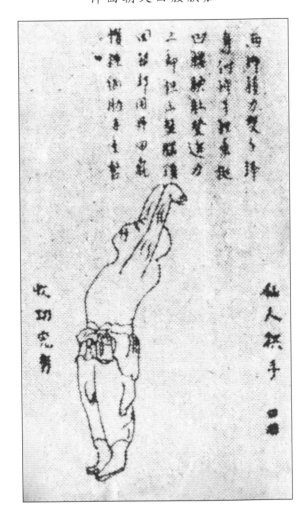

Practice Method

From the previous position, with the fists still touching the ground, change the hands to open palms and move them upwards as if lifting something. The head moves high and back, as if in a blowing wind. Then, with just a neck and head movement, first look upwards and then downwards, but do not move the head too far back or down. While standing in this upright position perform one complete breath.

When the standing and breathing are complete, bring the hands down alongside the body, and then visualize and sense circulating the qi and breath [at least two complete breaths].

Connect this last body position with the following exercise.

Second Exercise
Tyrant King Lifts the Cauldron
霸 王 舉 鼎
Ba Wang Ju Ding

Original Text

Place and press the palms of both hands together, held away from the body.

An eagle thrusts its wings forward so it can suspend itself in mid air.

When the rectum is closed off, rely on water and fire.

Both ears perk upwards when the sounds of the red cicada are clear and distinct.

It is important to completely rise and sink so that both kidneys are strengthened.

Bend the waist and lower the knees, but maintain lightness in the feet.

It is very important that students obtain the secrets of this active skill.

Constantly seek to increase and preserve the brightness of the mind.

First Movement
The Two Hands Separate the Water
Use Strength in the Two Legs
雙手分水兩腿掙力

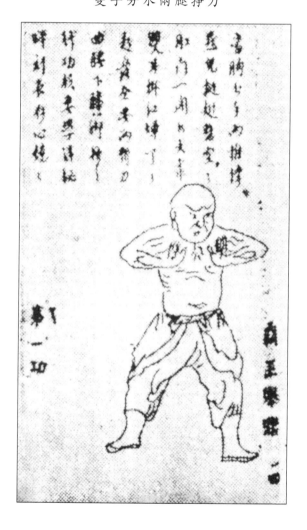

Practice Method

Position the feet out to the right and left, firmly placing them so that they are open, on line, and centered with each other.

Join the palms in front of the chest. Calm the mind so that the breath and qi can harmonize, slowly inhaling and exhaling while gazing directly to the front.

Second Movement
Two Fists Dividing at the Seat of the Pants
Remove the Saddle to Mount the Horse
雙捶分襠搬鞍騎馬

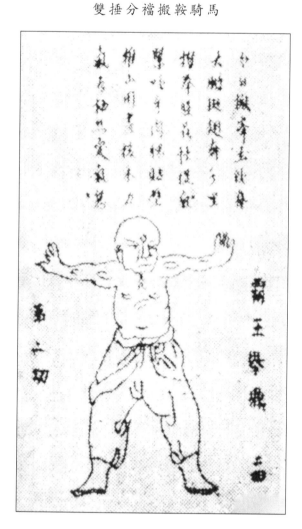

Practice Method

From the above position, and without changing the stance, move the palms outwards left and right respectively. Slowly extend them outwards and when fully extended, pause. When opening the arms outwards, exhale the qi.

When the hands are fully extended to the sides, position the fingertips so they are pointing upwards; when returning the hands to their joined position, inhale the qi.

Connect these two movements of opening out the hands and arms and then returning them for a total of eight repetitions, then pause.

Third Movement
The Great Roc Spreads Its Wings
Use the Strength of the Entire Body
大鵬挺肱全身使力

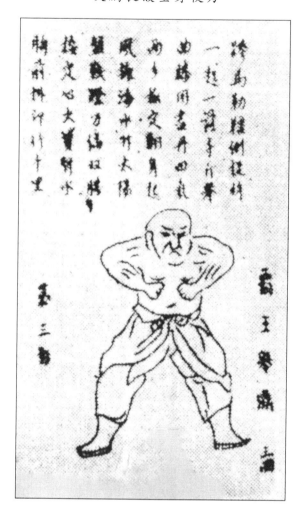

Practice Method

Without altering the stance, just change both palms into fists and punch them downwards and low to the level of the seat of the trousers.

Fourth Movement
Lift a Thousand Catties With Strength
Raise the Baton and Mount the Horse
力舉千觔提杵騎馬

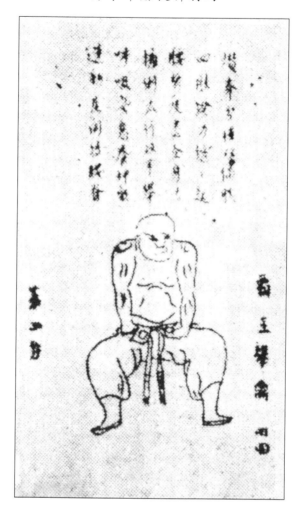

Practice Method

From the last position, open the fingers of both hands wide and then clutch them together into fists again, and with the palms facing the body as before. Once the fists are made, pull them upwards with the elbows on line with each other, and with both legs simultaneously extending upwards.

Repeat these motions [punching downwards and then pulling upwards] eight times. When the fists are punching downwards exhale the breath and qi; when pulling them upwards inhale the breath and qi.

Fifth Movement
A Golden Orb Encompasses the Moon
The Entire Body Is Strengthened by the Jing
Fire Refines the Golden Elixir
金盤抱月全身精力火練金丹

Practice Method

From the last position, change the fists into open palms and raise them upwards as if lifting something. The eyes gaze a little upwards when doing so. When standing with arms fully raised, inhale and exhale fully to circulate the qi.

Repeat these movements two times. Withdraw from the posture, pause momentarily, and then prepare your stance for the Third Exercise.

Third Exercise
Planting Flowers to the Left and Right
左 右 插 花
Zuo You Cha Hua

Exert strength to stretch the tendons.

拔 力 伸 筋

Original Text

Both hands strike the Jade Pillar to contend with Heaven, and appear like they are beating the Earth as they move together in unison.

Rising upwards brings fullness of the breath and qi and strengthens the muscles and bones.

The qi gathers in the joints and is directly and inversely affected by yin and yang.

Stretch open the three hundred sixty joints of the body, and the blood and qi will advance a person's strength.

Qian [☰] of Heaven and Kun [☷] of Earth conceal the Tai Yang [sun]. The Phoenix Spreads Its Wings and the clouds conceal the sun.

First Movement

The Two Hands Hold an Iron Saw and the Two Feet Are Equally Positioned

雙手扶鋸兩脚並立

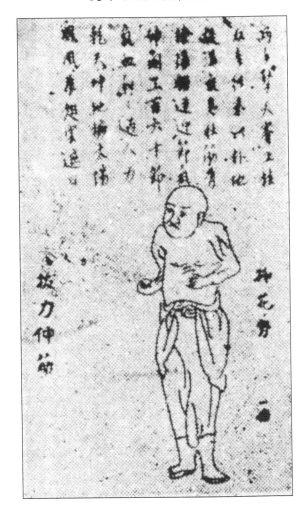

Practice Method

Stand upright with the feet together and make two fists, placing them on their respective sides of the waist with the elbows pointing to the back. Turn the head so the eyes gaze intently to the right side.

Open out the right foot so to be in a Right Climbing the Mountain Stance. According with the movement of the waist, change the two fists into open palms as they follow the stepping-out motion. One hand goes out long and the other short, pushing out to the right side. As the palms move outwards, the head and eyes turn to gaze intently towards the left direction. Exhale the qi.

Clutch the hands into fists and withdraw the right foot so to be in the original upright stance with the weight on both legs. This movement calls for inhaling the breath and qi.

First step out and then return the foot. Repeat these movements eight times in succession and then pause.

Second Movement
The Immortal Guides the Road
Mounting the Horse and Bending the Knees
仙人指路騎馬曲膝

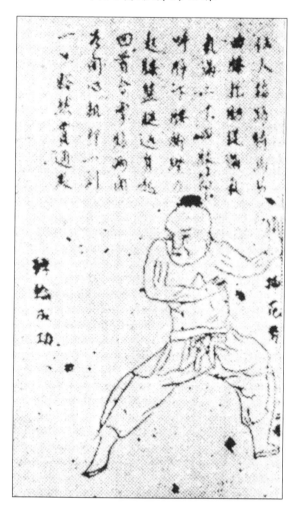

Practice Method

From the previous ending position of standing upright, turn the head and gaze intently toward the left.

Open out the left foot so to be in a Left Climbing the Mountain Stance. According with the movement of the waist, change the two fists into open palms as they follow the stepping-out motion. One hand goes out long and the other short, pushing out to the left side. As the palms move outwards, the head and eyes turn to gaze intently towards the right direction while exhaling the qi.

Clutch the hands into fists again and withdraw the left foot so to be in the original upright stance with the weight on both legs. This movement calls for inhaling the breath and qi.

First step out and then return the foot to the original position. Repeat these movements eight times in succession and then pause.

Third Movement
One Hand Passing Over the Brain
Compel the Qi to Become Substantial in the Abdomen
單手過腦偪氣實腹

Practice Method

The left and right feet change into an Eight Stance.[14] The left fist is raised high, with the palm facing out. The right fist is dropped low in front of the trousers, with the palm facing in.

---

14   This is called "Eight Stance" (Ba Stance) because the feet resemble the Chinese character and shape for the number eight (八, ba).

Move the arms as if the hands were pushing and pulling something upwards and downwards simultaneously. Repeat the movements eight times and then pause.

The inhalations and exhalations should naturally follow each other, so that when the left arm is being dropped down there is an inhalation. When the right hand and arm are dropping down, make an exhalation.

Fourth Movement
Hanging by a Hook, Embrace the Ribs
Bend the Knees and Reach for the Foot

垂釣抱脅曲膝勾脚

Practice Method

Stretch the right leg and foot outwards to the right side into a Right Seven-Star Stance. The left arm and fist are raised high, with the palm facing up. The right arm and fist are brought across the rib area as if blocking something, and with the palm facing in.

The entire body then squats downward and bends over towards the right leg, with the left fist extending towards the toes of the right foot and the palm facing in.

Perform these up and down movements eight times in succession. When moving upwards, inhale. When moving downwards, exhale.

Next, stretch the left leg and foot outwards to the left side into a Left Seven-Star Stance. The right arm and fist are raised high, with the palm facing up. The left arm and fist are brought across the rib area as if blocking something, with the palm facing in.

The entire body then squats downward and bends over towards the left leg, with the right fist extending towards the left-foot toes and the palm facing in.

Perform these up and down movements eight times in succession. When moving upwards inhale, and when moving downwards exhale.

Fifth Movement
The Two Hands Engage Together
With a Restraining Effort Raise the Qi
雙手交合收功提氣

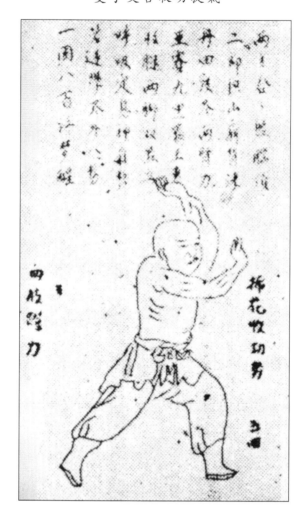

Practice Method

From the previous Seven-Star Stance, turn-step into a
Left Climbing the Mountain Stance. The left palm is raised
upwards [like thrusting into the sky] to the level of the forehead,
and with the palm facing the body. The right palm is brought
inwards to adhere to the inside and upper part of the left arm.
Stand and circulate the qi [inhale and exhale].

Like a rolling motion, turn the body to face the right side, and turn the feet to be in a Right Climbing the Mountain Stance. The right palm is then raised upwards to the level of the forehead, and with the palm facing the body. The left palm is brought inwards to adhere to the inside and upper part of the right arm. Stand and circulate the qi.

21

Fourth Exercise

Twisting the Roots of an Old Withered Tree

枯 樹 盤 根

Ku Shu Pan Gen

Reverse and circulate the Golden Elixir.

金 丹 還 轉

Original Text

The Rhinoceros Peeks at the Moon with both hands pushing out.

Turn the body, twisting the waist and chest, and step towards the front.

Perform a stealthy step to bind and hook and then press down on one knee.

One in and one out and then gather the two elbows.

Reversing the turn you must use the energy of the legs.

Raise the qi and close off the breath.

First Movement

Rhinoceros Peeks at the Moon
Both Palms Push Out in Unison
犀牛望月推送雙掌

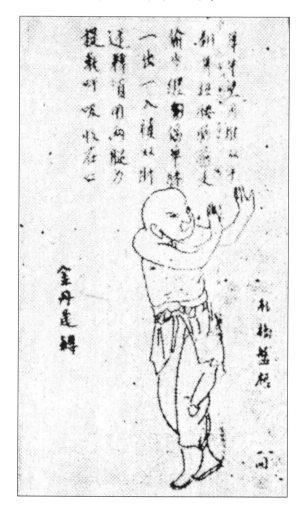

Practice Method

The left foot stealth steps towards the back and right side to complete a Stealth Step Posture. Both palms push out towards the right side, the right goes long and the left goes short. Inhale when stepping.

Both hands then change into a clutching position and are returned to left side of the waist area. When doing so, exhale.

One loosening and one tightening [of the fists] is performed eight times. Do this in combination with the movements [in photos 22 and 23]. When clutching the fists, use utmost effort in practicing this method.

Second Movement

The Hawk Turns Its Body to Repair the Inside of the Nest
Embrace the Fists

鷂子翻身窩裏抱捶

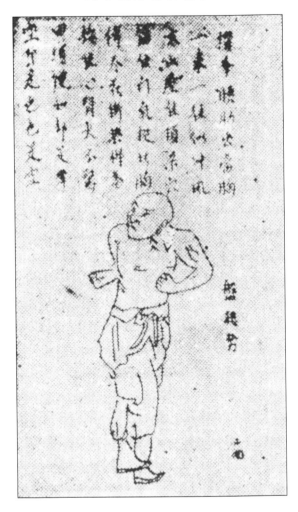

Practice Method

The right foot stealth steps towards the back and left side to complete a Stealth Step Posture. Both palms push out towards the left side, the left goes long and the right goes short. When stepping, inhale.

Both hands then change into a clutching position and are returned to right side of the waist area. When doing so, exhale.

Combine the movements [in photos 24 and 25] and complete the alternating of clutching eight times, then stop. Return to the [Four Levels] position of the first posture. This completes the practicing of the left and right sides.

Third Movement
Drag the Moon From the Sea Bottom
Bend the Knees and Lower the Waist
海底撈月曲膝下腰

Practice Method

The left foot steps around towards the right and back to complete a Stealth Stance in a low-seated Coil Posture. Both hands hang straight down. Using the shoulders, apply a gentle energy into the palms by shaking to and fro to the left and right, doing so eight times while harmonizing the breath.

26

Without changing the position of the hands, step around to the back and left side and perform the same shaking movement eight times.

Fourth Movement
Adhering to the Back of the Hands
Both Closing and Restraining Skills
背面手貼兩閉收功

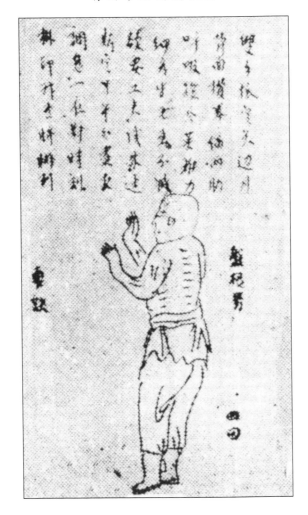

Practice Method

Place both feet together and hold the hands by the upper shoulders. Bend the elbows, with the palms facing outwards.

Harmonize the breath and stand a long time without moving. This is the method of Restraining Kung.

Fifth Exercise

Yaksha Searches the Sea

夜 叉 探 海

Ye Cha Tan Hai

Original Text

One action pressing down and the other action rising up.

One up and one down, then rise to restore the body.

The two legs are crossed to entirely use the energy of the sinews in the waist.

The Young Swallow Holds Mud as the body bends over.

The one square inch is pressed down and pauses to make one complete breath.

The two hands, left and right, separate up and down to open.

The entire body uses strength when passing over the head.

Close the eyes and fix the spirit by inhaling and exhaling the qi.

First Movement
Lifting the Cauldron With One Hand
單手舉鼎

Practice Method

The left foot moves back and passes over in stealth to the right direction, placed near and on the side of the right foot, with the toes of the left foot raised. Lift the right palm high. The left hand forms a hook hand,[15] with elbow bent, and is placed on the back.

---

15   *Hook hand* means to curl the fingers upward so to appear like a hook.

Second Movement
Bend the Knees to Pound the Ground
曲膝撲地

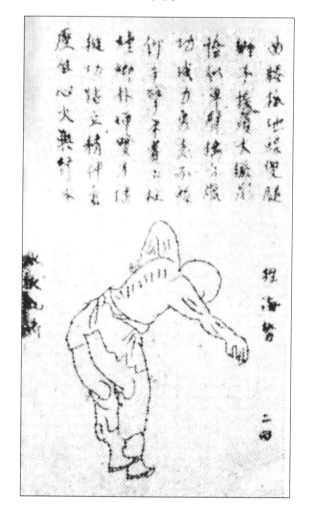

Practice Method

The entire body is bent over and down from the previous upright position. When bending, change the right palm into a hook hand. Move downwards until touching the ground and then pause.

Straighten the body. When rising, clutch the right hand into a hook hand and place it on the back. The left hand is changed into an open palm and raised high.

When raising the hand, an inhalation occurs. When moving down, exhale. These three movements [photos 29, 30, and 31] are repeated eight times.

Third Movement
One Hand Strikes
The Other Supports the Flank
單搥備脇

Practice Method

The right foot is moved back and passes over in stealth to the left direction, placed near and on the side of the left foot, with the toes of the right foot raised. The left palm is raised high, and the right hand forms a hook hand, with elbow bent, and is placed on the back.

Fourth Movement
Both Hands Hold Back the Leaking Water
把滲掬水

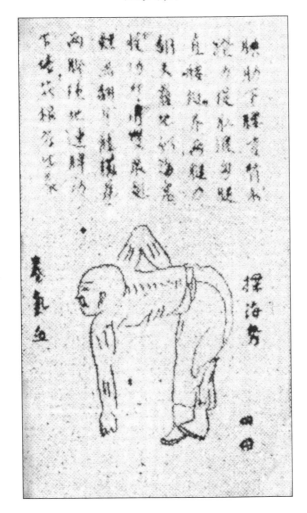

Practice Method

The entire body is bent over and down from the previous position. When bending, the left palm changes into a hook hand. Move downwards until touching the ground and then pause.

The entire body is then raised upwards. When rising, form the left hand into a hook hand and place it on the back. The right hand changes into an open palm and is raised high.

When raising the hand, inhale. When moving down, exhale. These three movements [photos 32, 33, and 34] are repeated eight times.

When finished, return to an upright stance to withdraw the posture [photo 35].

Sixth Exercise

Push Open the Window to Let in the Light

推 窗 亮 格

Tui Chuang Liang Ge

The sun and moon create the light.

日 月 生 光

Original Text

When crossing over, the energy should be as if pushing over Mt. Tai Heng.

The training resembles clashing against the wind or frisking a horse.

Return the hands to pull over the golden pagoda.

In all cases, long life dwells in every person.

Abstaining from wine and amorous encounters results in a wealth of qi.

The immortal Li Da endured having long eyebrows.

When you are able to circulate the breath, the yin and yang will circulate.

Heaven makes people, and so the body of a person is Heaven.

First Movement
Wrenching at Silver Pieces
While Moving Back and Forth
往來扭銀

Practice Method

Stand upright with both feet together and the two fists raised alongside the ribs [a Four Levels Posture]. The eyes gaze to the front.

Second Movement
Grasping the Tree to Push the Mountain
推山把木

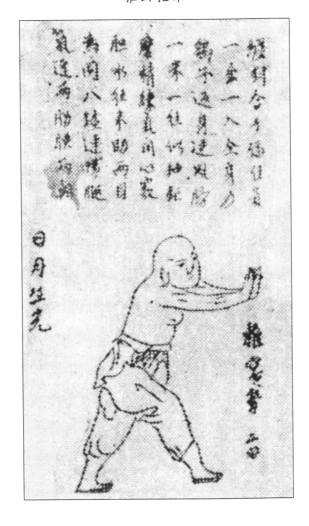

Practice Method

From the above posture, open the right foot to the side, then advance the left foot to perform a Left Climbing the Mountain Stance. The two fists are changed into open palms and push out towards the left side. Perform an exhale when doing so.

Then change both palms into intercepting hand positions as you withdraw the left and right feet [to the opening Four Levels Posture. Inhale during this transition of moving from one side to the other].

Third Movement
Raise the Net and Energetically Step
提網蹬力

Practice Method

Open the left foot to the side, then advance the right foot to perform a Right Climbing the Mountain Stance. Change the fists into open palms and push out towards the right side. Perform an exhalation when doing so.

Fourth Movement
Greet the Wind With Both Palms
迎風雙掌

Practice Method

Change both palms into Intercepting Hands, withdraw the left foot, and the right foot. Then return to the original position [photo 36]. Inhale when withdrawing [to the Four Levels Position], exhaling when advancing [to the sides in their respective Climbing the Mountain Stances]. Repeat these movements eight times in succession.[16]

[36]

---

16   *Eight times in succession* can mean counting the step to the left as "1," then to the right as "2," and so on. You can also count each repetition after completing all four movements so that you are stepping eight times to each side. This way of counting works for all exercises that move from side to side.

Seventh Exercise
Wei T'o Hands Over the Pestle
韋 陀 獻 杵
Wei To Xian Chu

Push energetically to complete the exercise.

排 力 成 功

Original Text

Draw up the spine to raise the qi and strengthen the sinews and bones.

The male and female Phoenixes dance, opening and closing tightly together.

Stretch the legs, unite the hands, and step out with full energy.

Push out to strengthen the chest like the pounding of thunder.

If attacking a tiger, best to [first] consider protecting long-life.

[If doing so] use diligent and strenuous effort of the four limbs.

First Movement
Separate the Hands in Front of the Chest
胸前分手

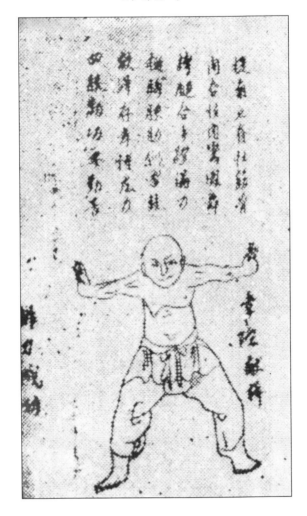

Practice Method

Both feet change and open up to form an Eight Stance so the heels of both feet are opposite of each other. The two hands are joined in front of the chest as though bowing before the Buddha. Circulate and harmonize the breath, gathering the qi into the Elixir Field.[17]

17   *Elixir Field* (丹 田, Dan Tian) is a qi center located three inches behind the navel.

Second Movement
Two Young Men Carrying a Mountain
二郎担山

Practice Method

From the previous posture, bring both palms out to the sides, opening and separating them, using softness yet combining it with a resistant-like strength. Exhale when doing this.

Third Movement
Raise the Cauldron With Joined Hands
合手舉鼎

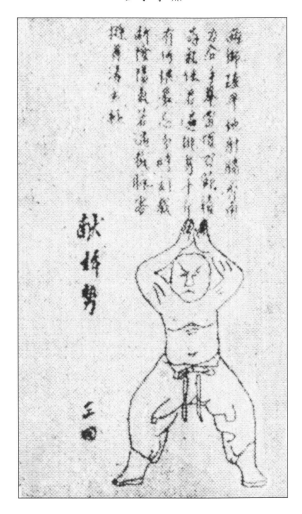

Practice Method

From the previous posture, maintain the original stance while bringing both palms upwards and clapping them together. Inhale when doing so.

Fourth Movement
Mount the Horse, Receiving and Closing
騎馬收閉

Practice Method

From the previous posture, with the two palms raised upwards move them down and separate them so they are open [as in photo 42], and exhale when doing so. [This is the same as photo 40.]

[Photos 39 and 40, 41 and 42] is to perform this movement one time, but complete [the sequence] eight times in succession before ending this kung.

Eighth Exercise

Old Buddhist Monk Enters Chan

老 僧 入 禪

Lao Seng Ru Chan

Original Text

Prop up the legs to make the ribs strong and gather the trousers to bind them tightly.

Illumine the mind to see the spirit, producing brightness in the eyes. Then the old Buddhist monk can sit in Chan correctly.

The wind twists the bamboo, creating shadows that illuminate through the gauzed windows.

One burning lamp, he blows on the lantern but does not extinguish the light.

In a vision he sees the Red Girl arriving in the West Chamber.

A board rests beneath his heart with selections written from the transmitted teachings.

The young Buddhist monk's nature is chaste but hard like bronze.

With determination through being unmoving, the work is done.

Why must one search the four directions to see the Buddha?

First Movement
Soaring Dragon, Crouching Tiger
降龍伏虎

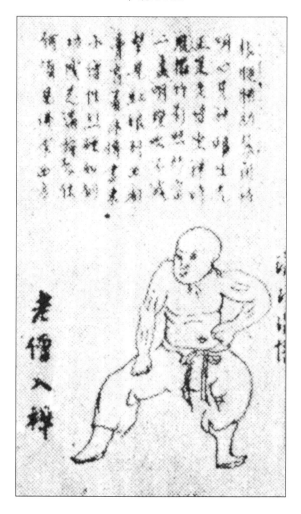

Practice Method

Stretch out the right foot, opening the stance widely. Then raise the toes like a Seven-Star Stance. The right fist faces towards the toes and the eyes glare at them.

Second Movement
Crouch Low to Fiercely Split
偪襠劈忿

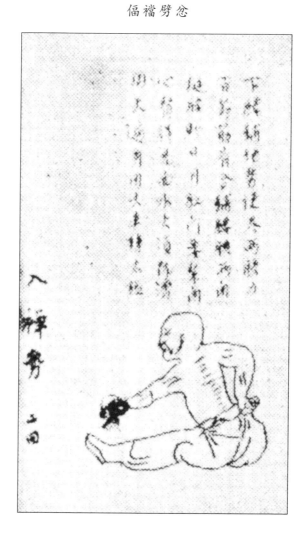

Practice Method

From the previous position, raise the body and change the stance by turning towards the left direction. The left foot and left fist completely turn to their opposite. Make this movement of moving left and right eight times. Harmonize the inhale and exhale when turning.

Third Movement
Separate the Trousers to Mount the Horse
分侷騎馬

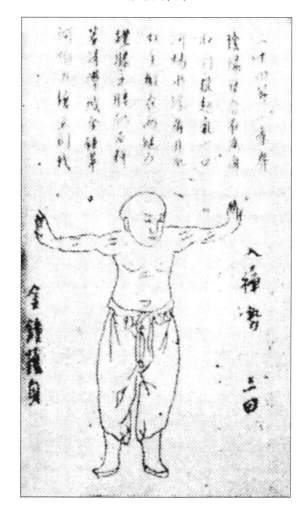

Practice Method

Both feet are brought together and the toes of the feet are opened so they each point out diagonally. The two palms are brought together in front of the chest with the elbows pointing straight out. This is all done with an inhalation.

From the above position, circle the palms out widely, left and right simultaneously, and exhale when doing so.

Combine these movements [photos 45 and 46] and make eight complete circular actions.

Fourth Movement
Two Swallows Flying
燕子雙飛

Practice Method

The feet are first opened up widely, as in a Horse Stance. The toes of the two feet are turned out diagonally. Both hands are lowered to knee level by clawing out and towards the inside. At the time of clawing, use the whole body in making the downward movement, and then as if seizing something, rise until straight, and then stop. Stay in this position for a while and harmonize the breath.

47

Ninth Exercise

Iron Ox Ploughs the Earth
鐵 牛 耕 地

Tie Niu Geng Di

Cut and polish your skills.

琢磨功

Original Text

Lower the screens and join the elbows to harmonize the breath and qi.

With the back upright the tongue rests above for support.

When yin overturns and changes into yang it is as delicate as silk thread.

The fire in the heart descends and the water in the kidneys ascends.

Within yin the yang is born, and within yang the yin is born.

Heaven, Earth, and the Ten Thousand Things are all of just one principle.

To produce the qi and blood, just practice the methods of this skill.

Moreover, these skills will strengthen the muscles and bones, and will invigorate the body.

First Movement

Stand Upright to Prepare the Cavities

並立備穴

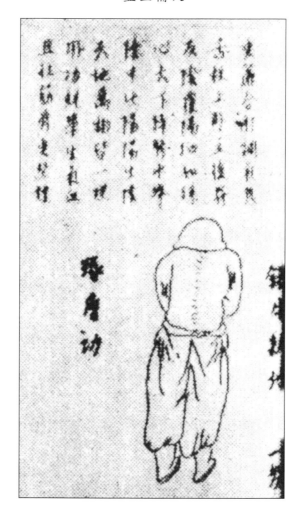

Practice Method

Bring the left foot around so that it crosses over to the back and right side, with the toes hooking against the outer right ankle and pointing upwards.

Bend the right arm at the elbow with a fist that faces palm up and has the intent of pulling energy. The left palm is brought over and across in front of the chest so the palm grasps the right forearm. There should be a feeling of resistance in the arms as though they have been struck and grasped, issuing a necessary energetic force. These actions all take place within the inhaling of the qi.

Second Movement
Use a Grasping Energy to Distinguish the Tendons
把 力 分 筋

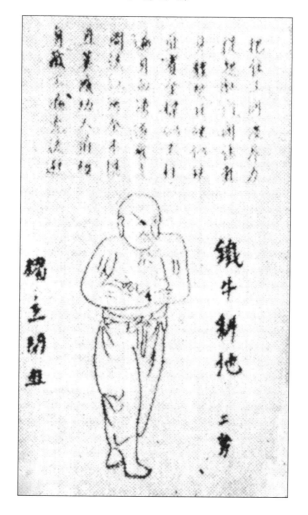

Practice Method

From the above position, move the hands and arms straight downwards by bending the waist over, with the arms joined. The right fist is directed down to point straight at the ground. These actions all take place within the exhaling of the qi.

Combine and harmonize the actions of these first two movements, repeating them a total of eight times.

Third Movement
Bring the Fists Together to Accumulate the Energy
攢拳積力

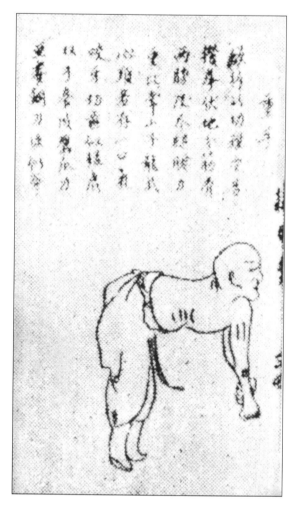

Practice Method

Bring the right foot around so that it crosses over to the back and left side, with the toes hooking against the outer left ankle and pointing upwards.

The left arm is then bent at the elbow with a fist that faces palm up and has the intent of pulling energy. The right palm is brought over and across in front of the chest so the palm grasps the left forearm. There should be a feeling of resistance in the arms as though they have been struck and grasped, issuing a necessary energetic force. These actions all take place within the inhaling of the qi.

From the above position, the hands move downwards by bending at the waist with the arms joined. The left fist is directed down to point straight at the ground. These actions all take place within the exhaling of the qi.

[Combine and harmonize the rising and bending over actions, repeating them a total of eight times.]

Fourth Movement
Fix the Breath Onto the Back
背面定息

Practice Method

To conclude, stand upright so that the feet are crossed in front this time. Bring the left foot and place it on the heel in front of the right foot and toes [photo 52].

The two hands form palms that are held like screens in front of the face.

Stand this way for several inhalations and exhalations so to harmonize the breathing.

Then change the feet so the right foot is on the heel in front of the left foot and toes, and stand facing the palms for several breaths.

Tenth Exercise

Green Dragon Wags Its Tail
青龍擺尾

Jing Long Bai Wei

Stretch the tendons to exert the bones.

伸筋拔骨

Original Text
With each elevation of the posterior keep the heart fixed.

Tightly grind the teeth together and then close quickly when raising the hands.

Left and right twist and turn the legs together at the same time.

The body resembles the turning of a stepping stone or the wind twisting the willow branches.

When the four limbs turn across, the abdomen should be full of qi.

Practicing this the knees and elbows are twisted together.

One coming in and one going out like the movements of double sabers.

When stepping to the front, pound the rear foot down, like a horse returning from a walk.

First Movement
Stretch Out and Push to Join the Hands
撐推合手

Practice Method

Open out into a Climbing the Mountain Stance with the left palm moving towards the right side with force and stretched outwards. The right palm draws down below the abdomen. Inhale the qi when doing so.

Next, bring the left palm in a downward circle and turn it upwards so it ends up over the head. The right palm moves slightly around until it is in front of the chest. At the same time turn so that the Climbing the Mountain Stance is changed into a Riding the Horse Posture. Exhale the qi when doing so.

Join the movements [of photos 53 and 54] and repeat eight times in succession.

Second Movement

Crack the Whip and Mount the Horse

揚鞭騎馬

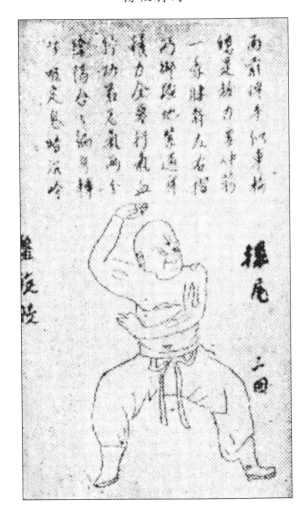

Practice Method

Open out into a Climbing the Mountain Stance with the right palm moving towards the left side with force and stretched outwards. The left palm draws down below the abdomen. Inhale the qi when doing so.

Next, bring the right palm in a downward circle and turn it upwards until it is over the head. The left palm moves slightly around until it is in front of the chest. At the same time turn so that the Climbing the Mountain Stance is changed into a Riding the Horse Posture. Exhale the qi when doing so.

Join the movements [of photos 55 and 56] and repeat eight times in succession.

Third Movement
In a Raised Stance, Bind and Seal
提步纏封

Practice Method
Open up the legs to complete a Riding the Horse Posture.
The right palm is out long and the left palm in and short.
At the same time turn towards the right side and use energy
pushing out. The eyes gaze to the right side.

Fourth Movement
Provoke to the Front and Protect the Rear
招前揚後

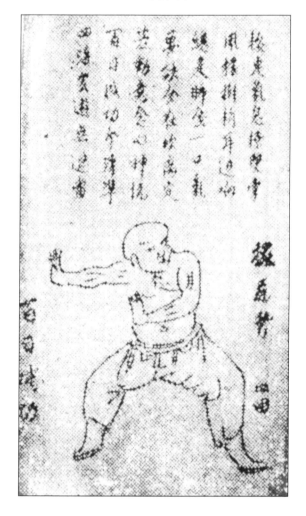

Practice Method

From the previous movement, remain in the original Riding the Horse Posture. The left palm is out long and the right palm in and short. At the same time turn towards the left side and use energy to push out. The eyes gaze to the left side.

Combine the movements [of photos 57 and 58] and regulate the breathing according to them. Repeat these actions eight times in succession and then withdraw to an upright position.

Eleventh Exercise

Left and Right Mount the Horse

左 右 騙 馬

Zuo You Pian Ma

Original Text

Bring up the waist and spine while standing upright with the hands held uniformly by the chest.

Rise three times and lower three times with a leg suspended in mid air.

On one leg, lift one thousand catties with strength.

The longevity of a crane is ten thousand years, yet the crane constantly remains youthful.

This will first strengthen the foundation through assisting the spleen.

How can obtaining the meridians and cavities unless there is a strong will to relax.[18]

Lower the waist so that the leg adheres and touches the ground.

It is truly amazing to ride the cart in this way, but before the work is completed a person must exhibit endurance.

Do not take this lightly for it will render you as strong as nine oxen and two tigers.

---

18 *Relax* (鬆, song). *Song* means to be "relaxed, alert, light, agile, and sensitive," in much the same way that a cat may appear to be sleeping, but is still alert to its surroundings. See my book *Tai Ji Quan Treatise* for more information on Song energy.

First Movement
Raise the Hands and Stand on One Leg
提手獨立

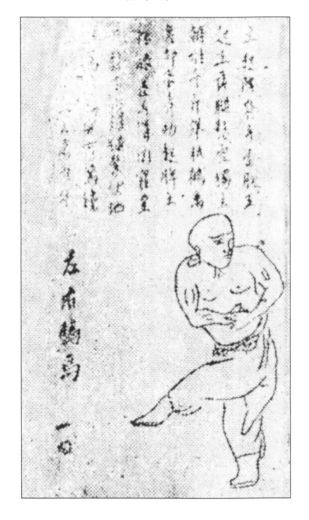

Practice Method

First, from the upright position, bring the right palm towards the left side in a crosswise striking gesture. When it reaches the middle line, position the left hand so that it grasps the right wrist strongly. Together they both move in line with each other with some exertion.

Simultaneously, the left foot is brought over to the right corner with the heel out, and when doing so keep the hands on line with the leg as they cross over. Inhale when making this movement.

Then with the heel still out, rise and sink [three times each] so the leg is just above the ground. After the third sink, rise [with the toes of the left foot touching the ground for better balance], and on the heel of the right foot turn the body towards the left until facing front.

Then bring the left palm towards the right side in a crosswise striking gesture. When it reaches the middle line, position the right hand so that it grasps the left wrist strongly. Together they both move in line with each other with some exertion.

Simultaneously, the right foot is brought over to the right corner with the heel out, and when doing so keep the hands on line with the leg as they cross over. Inhale when making this movement. [Then rise and sink as in photo 59.]

Alternate these movements [photos 59 and 60] eight times in succession [so that you end up performing the rising and sinking four times on each leg].

Second Movement
Step to Kneel at the Iron Gate
鐵門蹬膝

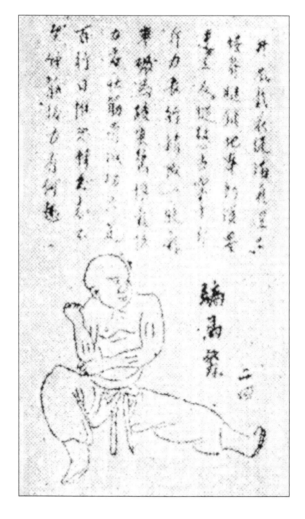

Practice Method

Bring the right foot out so that the stance is wide apart, only the toes of the foot are pointed up so to be in a Seven-Star Stance. The left fist, with elbow bent, faces up [with palm facing back] and raised slightly higher than head level.

Bring the right fist, with elbow bent, across and in front of the chest [palm down] to resemble a thrashing-like method.

Then bring out the left foot so that the stance is wide apart, only the toes of the foot are pointed up so to be in a Seven-Star Stance. The right fist, with elbow bent, faces up [with palm facing back] and is raised slightly higher than head level.

The left fist, with elbow bent, moves across in front of the chest [palm down].

Practice to the right and left sides eight times in succession. In the fixed positions exhale, but when turning inhale. Then stand upright and take a few breaths to calm the breathing.

Twelfth Exercise

The Swallow Sips Water

燕 子 啐 水

Yan Zi Cui Shui

Original Text

Replacing the rotting supports and columns by using the two hands to separate them.

One left and one right like two wings on the body.

Using a single power, make a complete step joined with the elbows and knees.

Raise the hands and drop the feet while twisting the muscles and waist.

Raise the Elixir Field through turning the waist and kidneys.

Only fear that the breathing and qi are not truly harmonized.

This is one complete kung fu with ten divisions of power.

Make shaking movements to strengthen the liver and to assist the golden lungs.

Why be anxious of a thousand or ten thousand affairs?

Just be diligent and careful in learning.

First Movement
Replacing the Rotting Supports and Columns by Using the Two Hands to Separate Them
抽梁換柱

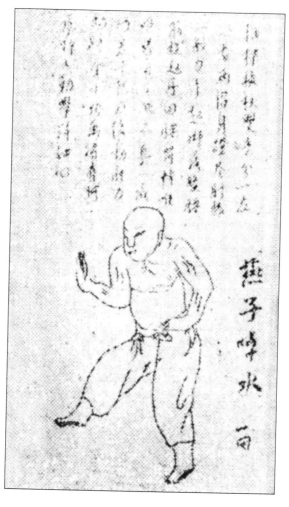

Practice Method

Pick up the left foot and stand on one leg [the right]. Both palms ate moved towards the back and are opened widely as if spreading wings.

Next, move the left foot over to the right side and putting it down into a Left Entering the Circle Stance. Bend the [left] elbow and place the left palm on the shoulder. The right palm then holds the left elbow for support.

Repeat these two movements eight times. Inhale when raising the leg, and exhale when stepping to the right.

Second Movement
Turn Around the Horse to Seize the Cicada
回馬捕蟬

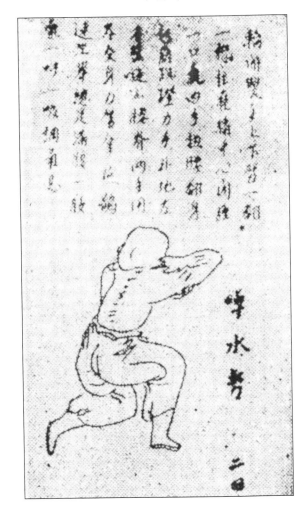

Practice Method

Pick up the right foot and stand on one leg [the left]. Both palms ate moved towards the back and are opened widely as if spreading wings.

Next, move the right foot over to the left side and putting it down into a Right Entering the Circle Stance. Bend the [right] elbow and place the right palm on the shoulder. The left palm then holds the right elbow for support.

Repeat these two movements eight times. Inhale when raising the leg. Exhale when stepping to the side.

Third Movement
Turn Over the Body to Join Hands
翻身合手

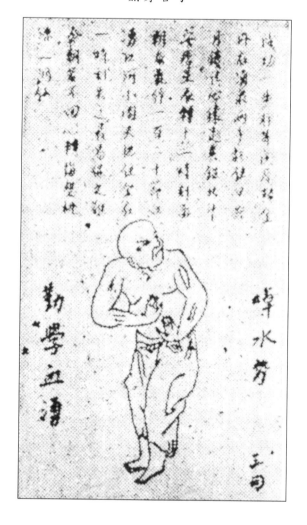

Practice Method

Stand upright with the feet placed together. Adhere the bent elbow and left palm to the waist, with the palm facing out, and position the right palm across the abdomen area.

Next, [turn the body to the right and] raise the left foot off the ground with the knee bent. The right palm is raised upwards, facing up and positioned levelly in front of the head. Place the left palm beneath the right armpit.

Combine these two movements and repeat eight times in succession. Perform the movements [in photo 67] with an inhalation and [those in photo 68] with an exhalation.

Fourth Movement
Golden Rooster Stands on One Leg
金鷄獨立

Practice Method

Stand upright with the feet placed together. Adhere the bent elbow and right palm to the waist, with the palm facing out, and the left palm positioned across the abdomen area.

Next, [turn the body to the left and] raise the right leg off the ground with the knee bent. Facing up, the left palm is raised upwards and positioned levelly in front of the head. Place the right palm beneath the left armpit.

Combine these two movements and repeat eight times in succession. Perform the movements [in photo 69] with an inhalation and [those in photo 70] with an exhalation.

After finishing the eight repetitions of this exercise, stand upright and take a short rest.

Thirteenth Exercise

Person Fleeing From a Tiger

虎 遊 人 身

Hu Ben Ren Shen

Original Text
Stand upright to fix the spirit and qi, standing still to establish
the root.

Raise the Bubbling Well through the palms of the feet.

Thrust forward the chest to make the ribs strong, closing
off the two kidneys.

Push out the hands, extend the tendons, and separate the
ten fingers.

Fill the abdomen by raising it so the whole body is strong.

Unite the yin and yang; unite the qi and blood equally.
Hollow the waist to make the stomach strong and push the
hands down to the ground.

Bend over repeatedly so to equally fold the sinews.
Circulate and Return to the Source, dividing the water equally.

Draw in and rest the Wei Lu, dividing the gold at the
source.

First Movement
Produce Wind From Both Sides of the Ribs
兩脇生風

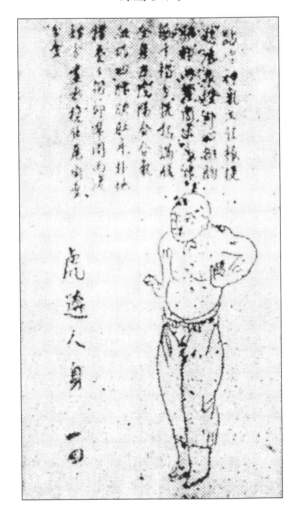

Practice Method

Place the feet together and stand in an upright position. While inhaling, lift the palms slowly, raising the elbows and palms slightly below shoulder height.

Second Movement
Four Pillars Suspended in the Void
四柱懸空

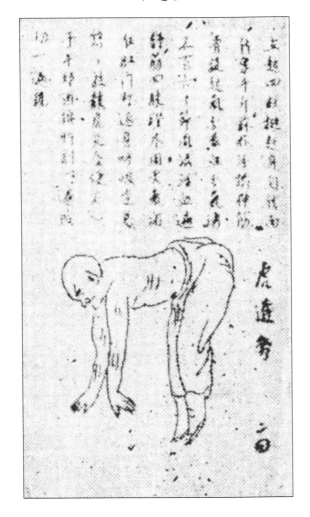

Practice Method

Exhaling, bend to lower the palms directly toward the ground.

Combine these two movements, rising and lowering, eight times in succession.

Third Movement
Dead Snake Lying on the Ground
死蛇榻地

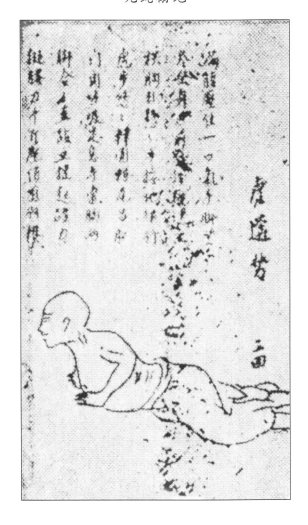

Practice Method

The entire body lies prone on the ground. Place the two palms and the toes of the feet on the ground, equally separated and opened with the head facing the ground, and exhale.

Then, using the strength of the arms, raise the body off the ground, with the head raised a little as well. Inhale while doing so.

Combine these movements of rising and lowering eight times in succession and then rest.

Fourth Movement
Hanging a Seal on the Front of the Chest
胸前掛印

Practice Method

Stand in an upright position with the two feet on line but with the toes turned out to the sides [as far as comfortable]. Raise the elbows and hands with the palms facing outwards. Circulate the breath and stand in this position as long as possible. Afterwards take a short rest.

Chen Tuan's Great Reason

陳 團 大 因

Chen Tuan Da Yin

Original Text

An old monk inquires about learning, but Chen Tuan sleeps.

With some tension raise the leg, the passing over of the knee is mysterious.

Fill the abdomen by raising and increasing the qi in the Elixir Field.

Bend the forearm and rest upon a pillow, content but annoyed.

Spread out the leg and lower the waist to position the back of the spine.

The sun and moon produce light in front of the eyes.

A Jade Rabbit ascends in the East, restored but not yet awakened.

A Golden Bird descends in the West, but still has not entered Chan.

Hardship and exhaustion are equally produced, yet nourish and accumulate when exhausted.

It is good to steal the flowers, but do not wait leisurely.

A determined will makes this kung fu great.

Yin and yang, separate the two, but do not hanker after them.

First Movement
Planting Flowers at the Bottom of a Well
井底栽花

Practice Method

Begin by standing at attention and then bring the right palm to be on line with the head. Withdraw the left palm under the right armpit so it is facing down and to the right side as if pushing out to the right. Simultaneously, stretch out the left foot to the back. Put all your attention in gazing to the right front direction.

Next, turn the body to the left side and take the similar stance, changing the position of the arms and legs to their opposite.

Alternate the right and left styles of this movement eight times in succession. Regulate the breathing according with the movements.

Second Movement
Grasp With the Fists
Split to Interrupt
攢拳劈岔

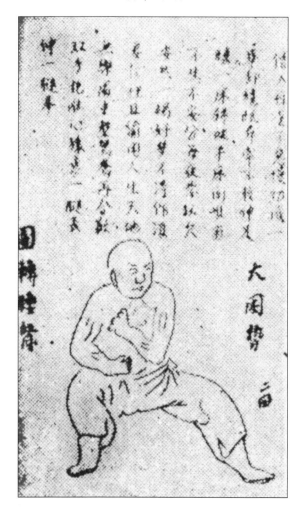

Practice Method
Stretch out the right leg to the side to complete a Striking Leg Stance. Position the right fist across the stomach horizontally to obstruct [palm facing down]. The left-fist palm faces the head with the elbow bent and the forearm held vertical so to perform a Striking and Thrashing gesture. Put all your attention in gazing to the right direction.

Next, turn the body to the left side and take a similar stance, changing the position of the arms and legs to be opposite.

Alternate the right and left styles of this movement eight times in succession. Regulate the breathing according with the movements.

Third Movement
Liu Quan Lifts a Gourd
劉全進瓜

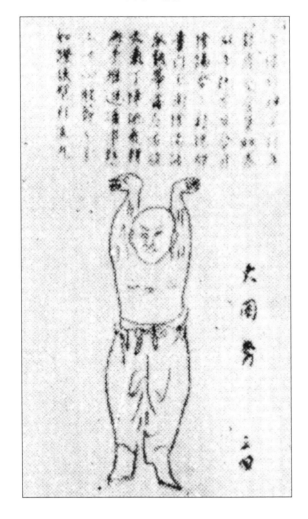

Practice Method

Place the feet together with the heels touching and toes turned out to make a Ba (八) shape. Raise both hands high [palms facing upwards], inhaling when doing so.

Fourth Movement
Use Energy to Swim Across the Water
浮水度力

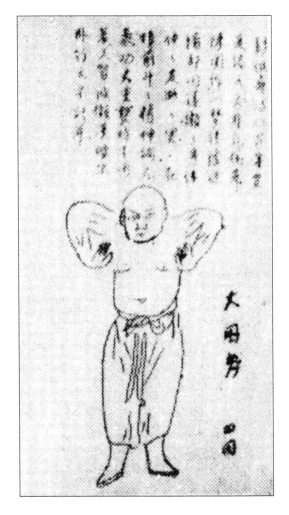

Practice Method

From the previous posture, bring both palms down while exhaling until they are on line with the shoulders, and then pause.

Repeat these rising and sinking movements eight times.

Fifteenth Exercise

Father and Son Requesting Rites

父 子 請 禮

Fu Zi Qing Li

Original Text[19]

Raise the qi, twist the waist, and snap strike with the palm.

Turn the body left and right with the ten families [fingers] moving quickly.

When completing this kung it must end very naturally.

When issuing out the energy it must be as if constrained.

Hold firmly the soles of the feet by squatting to make the energy full.

Imagine a circling to delicately turn the waist and kidneys.

This is learning how to distinguish both the yin and yang.

---

19   In the Chinese text, the father and son request to receive rites three times to expunge once with three words, but this is rare and strange language used in the original text.

First Movement
Turn the Body to Strike Out
返身撞捶

Practice Method

Bring the left foot around and behind the right foot, raising the left toes slightly. Withdraw the right fist and position it on the right side of the waist, with the left palm adhering to the shoulder along the right flank. Perform an inhalation.

From the previous gesture, make a wide step with the left foot out to the left side, completing a Climbing the Mountain Stance. The right fist strikes out directly towards the left side. The left palm then moves out and adheres to the right wrist. Perform an exhalation.

Repeat these movements eight consecutive times and then pause.

Second Movement
Holding a Thousand Catty Saber
把刀千觔

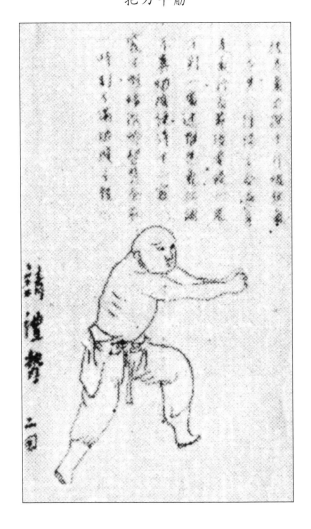

Practice Method

As with the previous movements [photos 82 and 83], perform the exercises to the right side [as shown in photos 84 and 85]. Repeat these actions [photos 84 and 85] eight times.

Third Movement
Turn the Body
Strike Out the Hands
返身扣手

Practice Method

Bring the right foot back and across to the left side while withdrawing the fists to the right side of the waist. Perform an inhalation.

86

From the previous gesture, turn the body to the right to complete a Climbing the Mountain Stance. The two fists strike levelly outward. Perform an exhalation.

Again, step with the right foot to return the body to the stance of the previous gesture [photo 86].

In combination with these movements [in photos 86 and 87], simply continue circling for eight consecutive repetitions and then pause.

Fourth Movement
The Great Prince Draws His Bow
霸王拽弓

Practice Method

In combination with the previous method [photos 86 and 87], turn [and step] to the opposite side to complete the postures.

Simply practice these movements [stepping and circling] eight consecutive times and then pause.

Sixteenth Exercise

A Carp Thrashing About
鯉 魚 打 挺
Li Yu Da Ding

Original Text

A thousand feet clutching the ground, moving forward and turning the body around.

Tread with utmost effort so the breath is strengthened, and so the blood and qi flow rapidly.

Hollow the waist to strengthen the belly, and to unite all the joints and bones.

Though the work is not yet fully complete, do not use forceful energy.

Although the body has stamina and is strong, it is without ease.

Circulate the qi and blood repeatedly to repair.

Use and follow these eighteen doors, but do not toil.

Each has a profound and wonderful solution, but they are not awakened.

The worthy master has not yet come to visit as a magnificent friend.

To summarize in one complete verse, "Constantly keep the mind in emptiness."

First Movement
Yellow Dragon Turns Its Body
黃龍返身

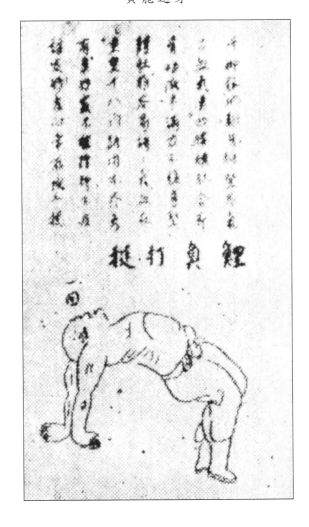

Practice Method

Place both feet about one foot apart. Bend the whole body backwards by the waist and torso until the palms of the hands are touching the ground. The knees, stomach, and chest should all be level and on line with each other.

From the previous position, bend the hands [and elbows] so the entire body is touching the ground. Perform an exhalation.

Then straighten both arms to raise the torso and knees. Perform an inhalation.

Repeat this exercise eight times in succession.[20]

---

20 Note: This exercise is very difficult and may be excluded from a person's regime. In kung fu practices, an exercise called "Cat's Waist" is used to train the body to perform this practice of *Yellow Dragon Turns Its Body*. To avoid any injury, a person should first train the Cat's Waist exercise before even attempting this kung, or forego this section of the exercise completely and move on to the other parts of this method. Since there is no photo of Huang completing this technique, one can't assume that even he could perform the second part of this movement.

Second Movement

Bend the Body
Draw the Bow String

曲躬扣絃

Practice Method

Place the left foot behind the right foot by hooking it around the right shin. Bend the right elbow and bring it up so the hand touches the back of the right shoulder. Support the underside of the right elbow with the palm of the left hand. Perform an inhalation.

Switch the leg position by placing the right foot behind the left foot, hooking it around the left shin. Bend the left elbow and bring it up so the hand touches the back of the left shoulder. Support the underside of the left elbow with the palm of the right hand. Perform an inhalation.

When changing positions perform an exhalation. Alternate the left and right sides eight times in succession.

Seventeenth Exercise

Zhang Lao Offers a Robe

張 遼 獻 袍

Zhang Lao Xian Pao

Original Text

Bring up the shoulders, push out the palms, and lift up one knee.

Thrust out the Bubbling Spring and turn the Wei Lu.

Close the Elixir Field by ceasing and holding the One Breath.

Open the spring of the two kidneys, and connect them to the spine.

When the qi is moved, the blood is sufficient. The work is complete when full.

In the four intervals make use of the work, then the mind will not be anxious.

Fix the breath of the inhalation and exhalation, the qi will then nourish the spirit.

Bend the knees and lower the waist, bending low and near the bottom.

First Movement
Raise the Knee to Embrace the Moon
起膝抱月

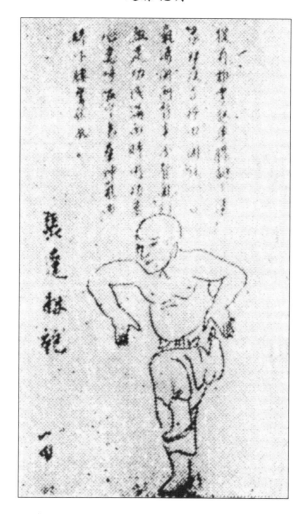

Practice Method

Raise the left knee to complete a gesture of standing on one leg. Both palms face the front at diagonals and opened wide, appearing like a bow being made in salutation. Perform an inhalation.

Next, bring the left leg down onto the ground, clench the palms into fists and withdraw them to the sides of the body at the waist. The right leg is then slightly stretched outwards and drawn to the rear. Make an exhalation.

Bring the right foot directly onto the ground and lift the left leg again.

Combine the movements of the these two gestures [photos 93 and 94] eight times in succession.

Second Movement
Energetically Step and Bend the Knee
蹬力曲膝

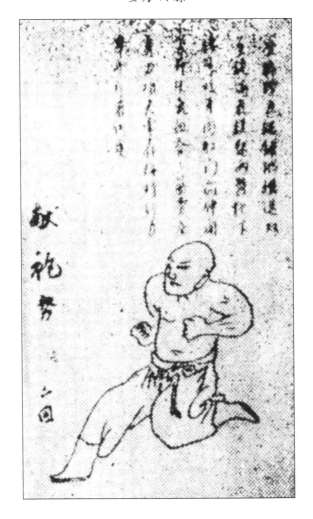

Practice Method

Repeat the above movements to the opposite [left] side [as shown in photos 95 and 96]. The movements, breathing, and number of repetitions are identical to the previous gestures.

Third Movement
Both Hands Cast Out to Forcefully Repel
雙搥硬崩

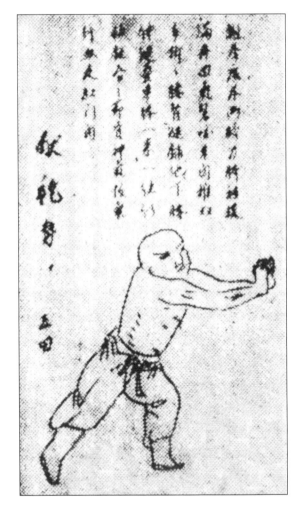

Practice Method

Open the right leg and move it to the right side to complete a Climbing the Mountain Stance. The two palms, levelly and on line, push outwards. Exhale the qi when doing this.

Next, turn and move out to the left side, completing a Left Climbing the Mountain Stance. When turning to the opposite side, inhale. The two palms simultaneously push outwards. Exhale the qi when doing so.

Alternate these actions from side to side eight times total, and then rest.

Fourth Movement
Mount the Horse and Rein in the Bridle
騎馬勒韁

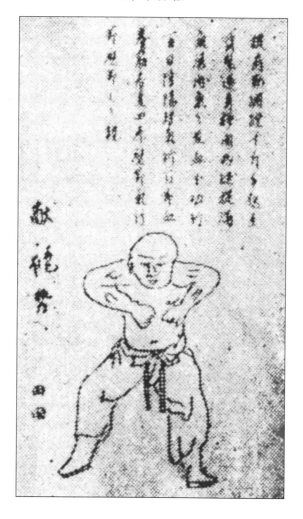

Practice Method

Position the feet to complete an "eight" [/\] shape, placing the heels to be on line with each other. Clench the hands into fists, with the elbows bent and raised to be on line with the shoulders. Harmonize the inhalations and exhalations.

Stand in this position until feeling tired. Afterwards straighten the legs for a short rest and the exercise is complete.

Eighteenth Exercise

Jar Hanging on a Golden Hook
金 鈎 掛 瓶

Jin Gou Gua Ping

Original Text

Half way into the evening make use of this skill if the body is fatigued. Initially settle the yin and yang by division of [the hours] Zi and Wu.

Harmonize and bring the qi and breath to fullness, with the legs joined at the shinbones.

Both hands hold up the sun for the spirit of the sinews and bones.

Stretch out the sinews to harmonize the qi. Nourishment is good cultivation. One turning over and one pushing out, both hands seizing.

Unstoppable, the heart is like a monkey and the mind like a horse.

If the qi responds with anxiety and muscular strength the blood will be insufficient.

Settle the square inch to nourish the spirit and qi.

Establish the gaze to get a good result and to accomplish this kung quickly.

First Movement
Fan the Eyes and Join the Shinbones
翹目交脛

Practice Method

Sit on the ground and place the legs straight out. The two palms [palm centers] are stretched up vertically like raising something upwards. When doing so, inhale the qi.

Second Movement
Fold the Body to Preserve the Kidneys
疊身存腎

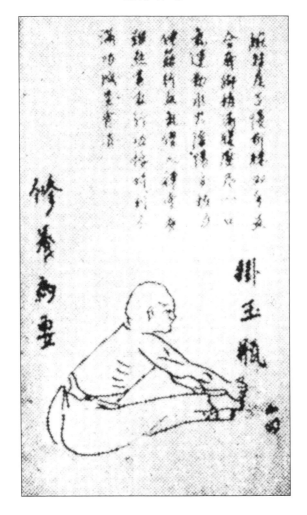

Practice Method

From the previous gesture, bend the entire upper body downward to grasp the feet. Lean the torso forward as far as possible [in your comfort range]. When doing so, exhale.

Repeat these first two movements eight consecutive times.

Third Movement
A Jade Pillar Supports the Sky
擎天玉柱

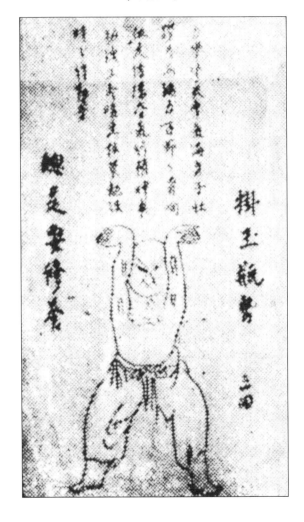

Practice Method

Position the feet to complete an "eight" [/\] shape, placing the heels to be on line with each other. The two hands [palm centers] are raised directly upwards as if supporting something high in the sky. Harmonize the exhalation and inhalation.

Stand in this position until tired and then withdraw from the exercise. This completes the execution of all the postures and movements [of the Eighteen Lohan Skills].

Part Two

Shaolin Lohan Skills

The illustrations and Chinese for this section come from *Lohan Gong,* considered to be the original Shaolin text of the Lohan exercises. This work only lists seventeen exercises, however, not eighteen. The first exercise in Fan Xudong's work *(Immortal's Hands in Salutation)* is not included in this text. Also, the ordering of the exercises differ from Fan Xudong's work, and minor Chinese character changes exist. Likewise, the drawings of the figures in the exercises are completely different from what Fan Xudong presented in his work.

First Exercise

Yaksha Searches the Sea

夜叉探海

Ye Cha Tan Hai

First Posture

第一式

一手偏脇一手舉
一上一下翻身起
兩腿夾盡腰節力
燕子啣泥身伏地
方寸按定一口氣
兩手左右上下劈
渾身使盡過頭力
閉目全身定氣息

Second Posture

第二式

攢拳頂脇兩扭腰
兩膀度盡勾樹梢
伸筋拔力生氣血
推動太極陰陽交
翻手合掌調氣息
功成一畢自然高

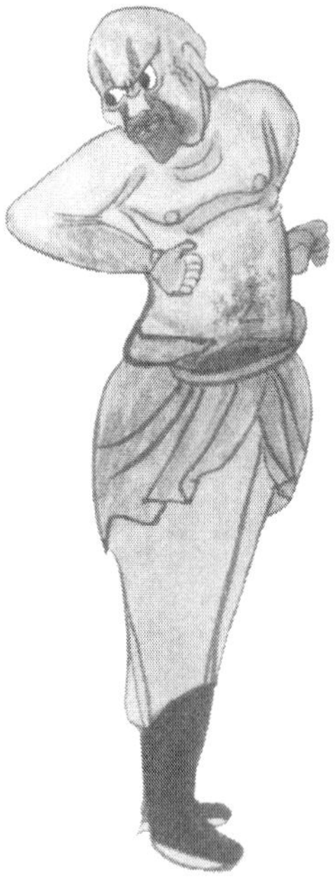

Third Posture

第三式

曲腰抓地膘雙腿
獅子搖頭大撅尾
惬似單臂擒方臘
功成力勇志不回
仰手擎天賽玉柱
螳螂撲蟬雙手擺
挺身踏定整氣力
按住心火運腎水

Fourth Posture

第四式

腆脇下腰滋腎水
撐力提肛纏勾腿
直腰兩脇挺盡力
翻天覆地似海龍
收功即用雙展翅
鯉魚挺身龍擺尾
兩脚踏盡一披地
土培花根花生蕊

Second Exercise

Push Open the Window to Let in the Light

推 窗 亮 格

Tui Chuang Liang Ge

First Posture

第一式

缠封合手偏住氣
一出一入全身力
鷂子翻身迎風旁
一來一往似抽鋸

精磨繡鏡開心竅
瞻水往來住身力
如同八踏連還步
氣盈兩脅腆兩臂

Second Posture

第二式

夜力推動太行山
學做衝鋒馬撒歡
回手拉倒黃金塔
豎立長存在身邊
能戒酒色並財氣
敢比長眉李大仙
若是調息陰陽氣
天作人身人作天

Third Posture

第三式

騎馬曳鞭手提繮
躥山跳澗總不忙
兩膀蹬盡全身力
身似玉柱腿似樑
二十四節蹬鐵壁
轉過泥丸放日光

Fourth Posture

第四式

順手推雙掌
纏封四平勢
推出天邊月
調息要還轉
養到氣血合
出手連聲響
提氣夾兩膀
還步轅門闖
一來即一往
自然筋骨壯

Third Exercise

Wei T'o Hands Over the Pestle

韋陀獻杵

Wei To Xian Chu

First Posture

第一式

提起立脊壯筋骨　挺胸腆脇似擂鼓

開合收閉驚鳳舞　欲得存養搏虎力

撐腿合掌蹬滿力　四時行功要勤苦

Second Posture

第二式
鳳凰展翅積竝肩
兩臂架住太行山
丹田氣滿挺腰脇
雙腿蹬定緊門關
按定神氣放心寬
何愁提捧遍身打
一旦豁然成功了
可以延年作地仙

Third Posture

第三式

兩腳踏平地
合手舉當頂
任君平身打
敢忘分時刻
若遇截脈客
肘腿齊放力
百節積滿氣
千斤有何懼
截斷陰陽氣
挺身湧太極

Fourth Posture

第四式
跨馬提脊兩分襠
雙手勒定意不慌
肘膝使盡滿腹氣
頭似鐵打身似銅
舉手最怕二還氣
面前生花卻難當
要訣全是養氣血
戒住房事有何妨

Fourth Exercise

Old Buddhist Monk Enters Chan

老僧入禪

Lao Seng Ru Chan

First Posture

第一式

掌腳腿腸緊閉襠　明心見性眼生光

正是老僧坐禪時　風擺竹影照紗窗

一點明燈吹不滅　夢想紅娘到西廂

膏肓着懷傳書東　小僧性烈硬如銅

功成志滿按不住　何必求佛到西方

Second Posture

第二式

下腰鋪地勢
使盡雙膀力
百節筋骨合
須要腿兩開
心腎得見面
水火須既濟
周天順身用
火車轉太極

Third Posture

第三式

二十四節一條脊
開合陰陽在尾閭
肛門提起一口氣
蝦蟆浮水躋井底
雙手搬住兩腿力
蹬膝立腰似石杵
若得學成金鐘罩
何怕鎗刀並劍戟

Fourth Posture

第四式
腿賽石柱兩手挺
自然而然氣力猛
走行常存過人力
單臂擎住千斤鼎
收成全要定氣息
兩腎水火似蟲拱
習成十八羅漢勢
敢比李遠下山勇

Fifth Exercise

Iron Ox Ploughs the Earth

鐵牛耕地

Tie Niu Geng Di

First Posture

第一式

垂簾合肘調氣息
舌根上豎立後脊
反陰覆陽細如絲
心火下降腎水舉

陰中生陽陽生陰
天地萬物皆一理
用功純熟生氣血
且壯筋骨更堅體

Second Posture

第二式

托住三關度盡力
提起肛門閉住氣
身似堅壯硬似鐵
亞賽金擦似玉柱
遍身血湧隨氣走
周流江湖全不懼
切莫成功人前顯
深藏不露凶徒避

Third Posture

第三式

抓住手腕挺兩臂
牽定鐵牛耕沉地
合手上下往來走
呼吸肺金一口氣
欲得功夫十二成
總是伸筋又拔力
整頓精神合氣血
一切收功照前行

Fourth Posture

第四式

欲行此功難受苦
攢拳伏地分筋骨
兩膀度盡腰腿力
就如坂坡趙子龍
咬牙切齒似猛虎
心頭常存一口氣
雙手學成千斤力
亞賽蛟龍出水中

Sixth Exercise

Green Dragon Wags Its Tail
青龍擺尾
Jing Long Bai Wei

First Posture

第一式

尾閭一舉存心口　四肢夌盡滿腹氣
緊咬牙關忙牽手　行時起膝好盤肘
左右盤環腿相隨　一來一往雙刀式
身似鐵鎖腿擺柳　前蹬後扑回馬走

Second Posture

第二式

鐵牛耕地似車輪
總是拔力要伸筋
一條腰脊左右轉
兩腳踏定緊隨身
積力全要養氣血
行功最忌房中事
陰陽交合出英雄
枉廢徒勞一片心

Third Posture

兩膀牽成一肢力
滿腹煉定一口氣
雙手擺尾快如風
曲膝撐腿腳踏地
遍身一百二十節
春夏秋冬按四季
陰陽一在分時刻
煉氣之時定鐘錶

第三式

Fourth Posture

第四式

按定氣息摔雙手
總是肺金一口氣
搖動肝木氣血廣
耳邊風擺樹梢響
要訣全在水火定
若動意念心學成
百天以後能準成
雲遊四海無擋處

Seventh Exercise

Left and Right Mount the Horse

左右騗馬

Zuo You Pian Ma

First Posture

第一式

立起腰脊手當胸
獨立朝剛千斤力
吸起脾土培根基
下腰鋪地緊伏腿
纏是功成顯人處

三起三落腿憑空
松鶴萬年皆長青
如得關竅豈肯鬆
能駕車輪實可驚
九牛二虎力非輕

Second Posture

第二式

井底栽花提滿氣
舉動須要連三及
常行積成一股力
氣虛力怯壯筋骨
惟恐轉意志不專
踏盡腰脊腿撲地
腿懸當空力千斤
車輾馬踏不甚畏
功成只在行百日
伸筋拔力有何取

Eighth Exercise

The Swallow Sips Water

燕子啐水

Yan Zi Cui Shui

First Posture

第一式

抽梁換柱雙手分　一左一右兩扣身

蹬盡肘膝一股力　手起腿落盤腰筋

提起丹田腰腎轉　惟恐氣息調不真

一成功夫十分力　搖動肝木吸肺金

千頭萬緒一口氣　時刻勤學細用心

Second Posture

第二式

輪開兩手上下劈
中心閉住一口氣
崩蹬跳力手扑地
兩手用盡全身力
總是滿腹一肚力
一翻一扠忙疊膝
回身扭腰翻身扣
左右盤旋立腰脊
鷹掌燕雀連三舉
一呼一吸調氣息

Third Posture

第三式

功成一步非等閒
兩手托定日共月
北斗安居星辰轉
氣行一百二十節
把住全在一時刻
今朝若不回心轉
圓轉金丹在湧泉
鎖住心猿是真傳
十二時刻面朝參
血湧江河小周天
失之最易得之難
悔想桃園二同仙

Fourth Posture

第四式

四肢搖動氣調胸
獨立起膝懸當空
猝開百節合筋骨
左右手起耳生風
若能兩膀千斤力
方可與人爭輸贏
身體受盡千般苦
切磋琢磨便成功

Ninth Exercise

A Person Fleeing From a Tiger

虎逩人身

Hu Ben Ren Shen

First Posture

第一式

踏定神氣立住根
挺胸腆肚兩腎閉
提起滿腹全身力
凹腰腆肚手扑地
周而後始分晝夜

提起湧泉蹬腳心
出手伸筋十指分
陰陽相合氣血均
摺疊疊摺節節準
挽住尾閭重分金

Second Posture

第二式

立起四柱挺身起
前扑後縱伸筋骨
氣湧三百六十節
四肢蹬盡周流氣
呼吸定息悠悠放
子午卯面按時刻
自然而然架千斤
提起氣分並血分
周流合血便舒筋
閉住肛門便翻身
龍虎交會使應心
一遍工夫一遍真

Third Posture

第三式

滿腹用盡一口氣
前扑後縱連三拱
依行虎步悠悠轉
呼吸定息手當胸
提起蹬力挺腰脊
手腿蹬盡全身力
胸脖懸懸手按地
圓轉尾閭肛門閉
兩腳合合竝站立
千斤壓頂有何懼

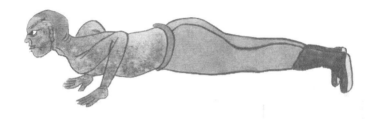

Fourth Posture

第四式

提起一口氣
用手雙抱月
丹田後氣滿
收功開雙手
氣血能調養
抖抖兩膀力
蹬膝腳踏地
擎天賽玉柱
攢拳貼兩壁
圓轉筋骨力

Tenth Exercise

Chen Tuan's Great Reason

陳團大因

Chen Tuan Da Yin

First Posture

第一式

老僧方學陳摶眠
滿腹提盡丹田力
鋪腿下腰立後脊
玉兔東升還未醒
若得志堅成功後

起腿蹬力膝懸懸
曲腕而枕休厭煩
日月生光在目前
金烏西墜方纏眠
陰陽兩分莫貪戀

Second Posture

僧入禪房不急慢
功夫一畢莫眠遲
尋常不敢伸腿眠
一床褥被半床間
莫使小僧不安分
每夜發狂久安然
雙手抱住心猿意
一腿長伸一腿圈

第二式

Third Posture

第三式

僧入禪堂不記年
雙手抱定日合月
貴門分開陰陽路
天龍下降地氣轉
二十四肢節節分
龍虎交會莫膽寒
陰陽合合雞抱卵
瓜熟蒂落左右旋
兩手推送頂梁懸
如蛇貼壁到泥丸

Fourth Posture

第四式

彭祖春活八百年
豈是俗人大非凡
總是陳摶作一夢
覆陰翻陽卻回還
抖抖精神調氣息
功夫重整時不閒
若人習成懶睡漢
坐臥立行不記年

Eleventh Exercise

Father and Son Making Three Requests for Rites

父子三請禮

Fu Zi San Qing Li

First Posture

第一式

提氣扭腰崩拳掌
翻身左右十字闖
終須自然功有成
何必勞力便勉強

挺挺腳心蹬滿力
轉轉腰腎細回想
陰陽滿兮有何慮
總是調氣要修養

Second Posture

第二式

拔盡氣力蹬千斤
陰陽交合遍身轉
一處不到一處迷
成功便得十二竅
智慧全在一時刻
吸其氣分應其心
氣行百節須要親
惟恐氣息調不真
一竅不明暗沉吟
不滿功成不回心

Third Posture

第三式

轉身回頭腳站立
扣住雙身提滿氣
扭腰崩錘忙掙腿
提步蹬盡全身力
左右回轉高拱手
下氣一定肛門閉
氣血合合筋骨強
十二時刻應節氣

Fourth Posture

第四式

回身拔力伸筋骨
曳弓撤絃須兩身
掙開兩腿氣要滿
氣行未到卻不均
遍身三百六十節
成功無力氣不真
分開陰陽調氣息
惟恐氣血調不真

Twelfth Exercise

A Carp Thrashing About

鯉魚打挺

Li Yu Da Ding

First Posture

第
一
式

手腳抓地翻身挺
蹬盡氣力血氣湧
凹腰腆肚合筋骨
功成不滿力不湧
身輕堅壯非客易
調調氣息再重整
十八門路用不盡
應心常存成一撚

Second Posture

第二式
抓墙貼壁似彎弓
仰面朝天氣挺胸
腳蹬滿地縱滿力
挽轉尾閭腰懸空
要訣總是養氣息
筋強骨壯方非輕
莫嫌此功無長處
能戒酒色速成功

Zhang Lao Offers a Robe

張遼獻袍

Zhang Lao Xian Pao

First Posture

第一式

提臂推掌起單身　氣行血足成功滿
挺挺湧泉轉尾閭　四時用力莫心急
丹田閉住一口氣　呼吸定息養神後
湧開兩腎串後脊　曲膝下腰緊伏地

Second Posture

第二式

提步勒韁蹬千斤
手起手落緊隨身
掙開氣分迸血分
功行百口陰陽轉
氣行百節血養筋
春秋四季應節氣
氣行隨應節節親

Third Posture

第三式

搬肩夜盡兩膀力
胯襠提滿丹田氣
緊咬牙關推雙手
摺摺腰腎腿鋪地
下腰伸腿疊單膝
一往一來似抽鋸
合和筋骨神氣壯
氣行百步肛門閉

Fourth Posture

第四式

疊膝蹬盡腿撲地
推送雙手提滿氣
提起兩腎忙下腰
緊咬牙關肛門閉
伸開百節生氣息
利了筋骨全身力
功夫常能按時刻
力舉千斤有何慮

Fourteenth Exercise

A Jar Hanging on a Golden Hook

金鈎掛瓶

Jin Gou Gua Ping

First Posture

何日纏能氣力足
心猿意馬鎖不住
一翻一折兩手扑
伸筋和血善修養
雙手閉目伸筋骨
調滿氣息腿交脛
期定晝夜分子午
半夜用功身勞苦
第一式

Second Posture

第二式
兩腳積力雙手捧
身似彎弓鯉魚挺
凹腰腆肚蹬盡力
二郎擔山盤腦頂
回轉卻用丹田力
攢拳伏脅再重整

Third Posture

第三式

當胸出手忙使禮
曲膝下腰緊伏底
氣如抽絲細細放
扣手閉氣翻身起
兩腳踏盡平生力
丹田還氣兩腎居
回手擎鼎雙抱月
開合收閉肺吸吸

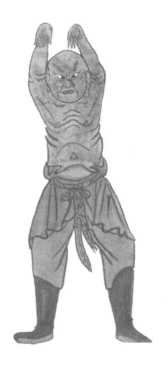

Tyrant King Lifts the Cauldron

霸王舉鼎

Ba Wang Ju Ding

First Posture

第一式

分水搬岸立後脊　　　緊咬牙關腮貼壁

大鵬展翅踔千里　　　推山用盡拔木力

攢拳盤頂忙提氣　　　氣如抽絲定氣息

Second Posture

第二式

當胸抱手兩腿撐
燕子挺翅懸當空
肛門一閉水火兼
雙耳卦紅單丁丁
起落全要兩腎力
曲騰下腰腳輕輕
行功若要學得力
時刻存心常兢兢

Third Posture

第三式

攢拳分襠雙偈膝
四肢登力悠悠起
腰肩虛盡全身力
擁倒泰山雙手舉
吸呼定息精神氣
運動尾閭轉腰脊

Fourth Posture

第四式

跨馬勒韁倒提杆
一起一落千斤力
曲膝用盡丹田氣
兩手抓定翻身起
風擁海水太陽升
盤鞍捶蹬偏雙膝
按定心火滋腎水
胸前挂印行千里

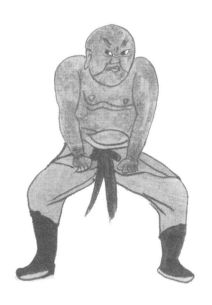

Fifth Posture

第五式

兩手擎天賽玉柱
雙手往來似撲地
提滿氣息壯筋骨
陰陽順送應節氣
伸開三百六十節
氣血合和過頂力
乾天坤地擁太陽
鳳凰展翅雲遮日

Sixteenth Exercise

Planting Flowers to the Left and Right

左右插花

Zuo You Cha Hua

First Posture

第一式

仙人指路騎馬勢　　吸肺下腰脚蹬力

曲膝抱脇提滿氣　　提膝盤腿翻身轉

氣滿二十四支節　　回手合掌貼兩壁

Second Posture

第二式

單手至腦取腳稍
提氣駢脇慢下腰
曲膝蹬盡全身力
智深拔柳萬丈高
挺胸腆肚偪雙拳
反手合掌立樹苗
滿腹度盡千斤力
氣如抽絲陰陽交

Third Posture

第三式

兩手交合盤腦頂
二郎擔山肩臂聳
丹田皮盡兩腎力
亞賽霸王九里勇
收腿兩腳雙並立
吸呼定息神氣整
若還學盡十八勢
一睡八百纔夢醒

Fourth Posture

第四式

舉山拔木過頭力
積成骿脇一口氣
左右皆同是一樣
陰陽皆安轉太極
功成全憑子午定
鐵打屋樑立腰脊

Seventeenth Exercise

Twisting the Roots of an Old Withered Tree

枯樹盤根

Ku Shu Pan Gen

First Posture

第一式

犀牛望月推雙手
翻身扭腰胸前走
偷步纏勾偏單膝

一出一入積雙肘
還轉須用兩腿力
提氣呼吸收在口

Second Posture

第二式

攢拳腆脇手當胸
一來一往似冲鋒
太山壓住頂撑穴
閉住肛門氣挺胸
穿盡花街入柳巷
按住心火腎不驚
回頭便知卻是岸
空即是色色是空

Third Posture

第三式

雙手抓定天邊月
背面攢拳偪兩脇
吸呼蹬進英雄力
細如牛毛吹不滅
欲求功夫急速成
期定子午分晝夜
調息一在對刻數
挂印升座將挑列

Fourth Posture

第四式

海底撈月對胸膝
兩手撲地管一尺
鼻內抽絲一口氣
轉身扭腰悠悠起
金盤托住劉全進
兩腳踏定立腰脊

Part Three
Buddhist Eighteen Lohan Figures

This section examines the characteristics of the Eighteen Lohans, presenting an image associated with each individual, their Sanskrit, Chinese, and English names, as well as a brief verse and background information on each one. In Theravada Buddhism, the Arhat (Arahat or Arahant—"Lohan" in Chinese) is one who follows the Eightfold Path and so achieves enlightenment. In their view, Arhats are Buddhas, but since there can only be one Buddha in the world, those who find enlightenment after him are called Lohans (Arhats).

Lohans are known for their great wisdom, bravery, and supernatural powers. Because of their abilities to ward-off demons and evil spirits, Lohans are considered guardians of Buddhist temples and are usually seen in a temple's main hall standing guard. They appear indomitable and even fierce looking to scare off any demonic influences. In Xiang Shan (Fragrant Hills) Temple in China, for example, the major Eighteen Lohans are accompanied by five hundred statues of other lesser Lohans.

Images of the Lohans were first created by the Buddhist monk Guan Xiu in 891 CE. Guan Xiu was from Chengdu in Sichuan province. Guan was said to have been exceptionally adept in his scholarly studies of painting, calligraphy, and poetry —the three necessary skills of any Chinese artist. Because of his expert painting skills, legends say, the Lohans decided to have him paint their portraits, and so they appeared to him in his dreams so he could fulfill their request. Interestingly, Guan Xiu claimed that the order of the Eighteen Lohans was not based on their spiritual strength or rank, rather the order in which they appeared in his dreams, and that their ranks were all equal to each other, even though each had different spiritual skills, or penetrations.

Since the time of Guan Xiu (Tang dynasty), numerous Chinese painters, sculptors, and potters have sought to bring these legendary figures to life, and many of them based their portrayals of the Lohans on Guan Xiu's original paintings.

The text of the verses and stories provided in this section were most likely originally taken from *The Record of the Duration of the Dharma* (法住記, *Fa Zhi Ji*), even though no citation for this text appears in any of the Chinese sources used in the translations for this section. The *Fa Zhi Ji* was supposedly spoken by the Great Arhat Nadimitra, and translated by Xuanzang, the famous Chinese Buddhist monk who traveled to India to collect sutras and other works in 654 CE. When and where the inclusion of the last two Arhats, *Taming Dragon* and *Taming Tiger*, originated from is unknown, but they may have been a Buddhist appropriation of Daoist figures, as these Arhats have been represented as immortals in some Daoist circles.

Deer Sitting Lohan

騎鹿羅漢

Pindola the Bharadvaja

Sitting dignified on a deer,
As if in deep thought.
With perfect composure,
Content with being
above worldly pursuits.

Pindola the Bharadvaja, from a high caste Brahmin family, was formerly a powerful government official in an Indian kingdom, highly trusted by the king. One day he suddenly decided to become a Buddhist monk and, not wanting to hear any entreaties from the king, he left to join a monastery deep in the mountains.

One day, he appeared in front of the palace, riding a deer. Recognizing him, the royal guards immediately reported to the king who came out to receive him. The king told him that he could have his position back if he wanted. Bharadvaja declined and said that he came back to ask the king to join him. After a long conversation, using various metaphors to explain the sins of the flesh and desires, he finally convinced the king, who abdicated in favor of his son and followed Bharadvaja to become a monk.

Happy Lohan

喜慶羅漢

Kanaka the Vatsa

Decimating the demons,
The universe now cleared.
Hands raised for jubilation,
Be wild with joy.

Kanaka the Vatsa was a well-known public speaker and debater of Buddhist doctrines. When asked "What is happiness?" he would answer that it is experienced through the five senses. When asked "What is bliss?" he would reply that bliss is joy coming not from the five senses but from deep within, like feeling Buddha in his heart. He often wore a smiling countenance during debates and was famous for his preachings on happiness, therefore he is called the Happy Lohan.

Raised Bowl Lohan

舉
鉢
羅
漢

Kanaka the Bharadvaja

In majestic grandeur,
Joy descends from heaven.
Raised the bowl to receive happiness,
Glowing with jubilance and exultation.

Kanaka the Bharadvaja was a Buddhist mendicant monk who used to ask for alms by raising his bowl. After he had attained enlightenment, he was called the Raised Bowl Lohan. The word alms bowl, *bo,* was borrowed from Sanskrit, taking the first of the three syllables of the original word, because there was no such word in Chinese. In the very beginning, the bowl was made of metal. Nowadays, the bowl is commonly found to be made of finely polished halves of coconut shells or red beech wood. Its use of holding alms food remains unchanged.

Raised Pagoda Lohan

托塔羅漢

Nandimitra

A seven story pagoda,
Miraculous power of the Buddha.
Forceful without being angry,
With preeminent Buddhist might.

According to legend, this Lohan, Nandimitra, the sweet one, was the last disciple of the Buddha. In memory of his dear beloved master, Nandimitra often carried a specially made pagoda with him, signifying that Buddha was always there, forever.

Before the introduction of Buddhism to China, no pagodas existed in the country. The Chinese had to create a new character, from the first syllable of the original Sanskrit word, to call this unique architectural structure. In Buddhism, the pagoda is a container for the Buddha's bones, and, therefore, symbolizes the faith.

Meditating Lohan

靜座羅漢

Nakula

Quietly cultivating the mind,
A countenance calm and composed.
Serene and dignified,
To enter the Western Paradise.

According to tradition, this Lohan, Nakula or Pakula, was originally a warrior with immense strength. He gave up the life of fighting and killing to become a monk, finally attaining enlightenment through constant meditation. However, due to his former profession, he still exuded much physical strength even during meditation. In mythology, this Lohan's sphere of influence extended through all of India, and he was considered one of Buddha's favorite disciples. Occasionally, he is portrayed as a teacher, holding a string of Buddhist rosary with a small boy beside him.

Overseas Lohan

過
江
羅
漢

Bodhidruma

Bearing the sutras,
Sail east to spread the dharma.
Climbing mountains and fording streams,
For the deliverance of humanity.

Bodhidruma in Sanskrit means virtuous and sagacious. It is also the name of a rare tree in India, the bodhi, which has became famous and known as the tree of wisdom because Sakyamuni became enlightened under its shade. This Lohan was born under such a tree and was given the name of Bodhidruma. Legend has it that Bodhidruma was responsible for spreading Buddhism to the East Indies. From India he sailed across the ocean to land on the island of Java, hence the name "Overseas."

Elephant Riding Lohan

騎象羅漢

Kalika

Riding an elephant with a dignified air,
Chanting aloud the sutras.
With a heart for humanity,
Eyes scanning the four corners of the universe.

Kali in Sanskrit means elephant and *kalika,* an elephant rider, or "a follower of kali." The elephant, for its immense strength and power, endurance, and perseverance, symbolizes Buddhist might. Kalika the Lohan was an elephant trainer turned Buddhist monk who had earned sufficient merits to attain enlightenment. In memory of his former profession, he is often portrayed with an elephant.

Laughing Lion Lohan

笑獅羅漢

Vajraputra

Playful and free of inhibitions,
The lion cub leaps with joy.
Easily alternating tension with relaxation,
Rejoicing with all living things.

Vajraputra literally means "man of cats." He was a lion hunter before he was converted to Buddhism. After he had attained enlightenment, a little lion came playfully to his side. The animal seemed to be grateful to him for giving up the life of killing lions, thus sparing its parents and brothers. Since then, Vajraputra and the little lion have become inseparable. The lion, with its earthshaking roar, symbolizes the invincible might of Buddhism. Therefore, it's common to find a pair of lions standing guard at the front gate of a Buddhist temple or monastery in China.

Open Heart Lohan

開
心
羅
漢

Gobaka

Open the heart and there is Buddha,
Each displaying his prowess.
The two should not compete,
For Buddha's power is boundless.

Gobaka was the prince of a minor kingdom in India. When he was made crown prince, his younger brother started a rebellion. Gobaka assured his brother, however, that he wanted to refuse the kingdom and become a monk because he only had Buddha in his heart. As proof, he exposed his chest and there indeed was a Buddha in his heart. The younger brother then believed him and stopped the rebellion. Gobaka became a monk. It is believed that Gobaka was the monk Shan Wu Wei, who arrived at Changan (today's Xian) during the Tang Dynasty in 716 CE. Gobaka literally means "man of heart," weak physically but strong of spirit.

Raised Hand Lohan

探手羅漢

Pantha the Elder

Easy and comfortable,
Yawning and stretching.
In a state of omniscience,
Contented with his own lot.

According to legend, Pantha the Elder was the prince of a small Indian kingdom called Kintota. When he became a monk, he liked to meditate in the half-lotus style. Upon waking up, he would raise his hands and let out a deep breath, hence the name Raised Hand. He was the elder brother of the Doorman Lohan. The two brothers were both born while the mother was traveling, and were given a Sanskrit name which means "born on the road."

Thinking Lohan

沉思羅漢

Rahula

Pondering and meditating,
Understanding it all.
Above this world and free from conventions,
Compassion conveyed up to the Ninth Heaven.

Rahula is the Indian name of a constellation. In ancient India, it was believed that eclipses were caused by a star coming between the Earth and the moon or the sun; blocking out the light. This Lohan was born during a lunar eclipse and was given the name Rahula, the constellation that caused this phenomenon. Rahula was one of the Buddha's ten favorite disciples, and was well-known for his meditative power. It is believed that he could become omnipotent and omniscient during meditation. When deep in thought, he was ruminating on wisdom and action.

Ear Scratching Lohan

挖耳羅漢

Nagasena

Leisurely and content,
Happy and knowledgeable.
Full of wit and humor,
Exuberant with interest.

His Sanskrit name is Nagasena, which means an "army of dragons" and symbolizes strong supernatural power. Nagasena was an eloquent speaker and debater. He was famous all over India for his preachings on the maxim of "hear no evil." The sense of hearing is one of the six sources through which humans become aware of the world. Therefore a practitioner of Buddhism should avoid listening to decadent sounds and in particular other people's secrets. Thus he is often portrayed as scratching his ear, a gesture symbolizing the purification of the sense of hearing in the search for peace.

Calico Bag Lohan

布袋羅漢

Angida

Buddha of infinite life,
Valuable bag containing
secrets of Heaven and Earth.
Happy and contented,
Cheerful and joyful is he.

According to legend, Angida was an Indian snake-catcher whose aim was to prevent the snakes from biting passersby. After the snakes were caught, he would remove the venomous fangs and then release them in the mountains. It was due to this kindness of heart that Angida was able to attain enlightenment. He carried a bag in which to put the snakes.

He is supposed to have appeared in Fenghua in Zhejiang Province in 907 CE as a mendicant monk carrying a bag. He was seen for the second time in China in 917 CE, preaching on a rock next to the Yuelin Temple.

Plantain Lohan

芭蕉羅漢

Vanavasa

Carefree and leisurely,
Disdainfully regards the Great Void.
With celestial airs and religious spirit,
Transcending this mortal world.

According to legend, this Lohan was born during a heavy downpour, and the plantain trees in his back garden were rustling noisily. Thus he was named Vanavasa, which means "rain" in Sanskrit. Later on he became a Buddhist monk, finally attaining enlightenment. Because he liked to meditate under a plantain tree, he is called the Plantain Lohan. In mythology, he is supposed to have been stationed on the Ko-Chu Mountain with fourteen hundred lesser Lohans. He is sometimes shown meditating in a cave with eyes closed and hands folded over his knees.

Long Eyebrow Lohan

長眉羅漢

Asita

Compassionate elder,
A monk who has attained enlightenment.
Perceptive of the infinite universe,
With tacit understanding.

Asita in Sanskrit means incomparably proper, or of correct proportions in spirit and physique. According to legend, Asita was born with two long white eyebrows. The story was that in his previous life he was a monk who, though having tried very hard, could not attain enlightenment, even at a ripe old age, so he had only two long white eyebrows left. After his death he reincarnated again as a human being. After he was born, his father was told that Shakyamuni Buddha also has two long eyebrows, therefore his son had the look of the Buddha in him. As a result, Asita was sent away to a monastery to become a monk, eventually attaining enlightenment.

Doorman Lohan

看門羅漢

Pantha the Younger

Powerful, husky and tough,
Watching with careful alertness.
With the Buddhist staff in hand.
Valiantly annihilates the evil.

According to legend, this Lohan, also known as Pantha the Younger, was one of Buddha's favorite disciples. When he went begging for alms, he would bang on people's doors. One time he did that, the old and rotten door fell apart, and he had to apologize to the owner of the house. So Buddha gave him a tin staff and told him, "When you go alms begging, you don't have to bang on people's doors any more. Just tap this staff. If the people inside want to give you alms, they will come out." The tin staff had several rings on it and made a light noise when tapped. The tin staff has become the symbol of this Lohan.

Taming Dragon Lohan

降龍羅漢

Nantimitolo

In the hands are the spiritual pearl and the holy bowl,
Endowed with power that knows no bounds.
Full of valor, vigor, and awe-inspiring dignity,
To succeed in vanquishing the ferocious dragon.

His Sanskrit name is Nantimitolo. *Nanti* means happy, and *mitolo,* friend. Together the name means "happy friend." He is called the Taming Dragon Lohan for a brave act he performed. In ancient India, the people of a small kingdom, after being incited by a demon, went on a rampage against the Buddhists and monasteries, stealing Buddhist sutras. The king of the undersea flooded the kingdom and rescued the sutras, which he put in his palace. Nantimitolo subdued the dragon guard and restored the sutras to earth. Hence he is called the Taming Dragon Lohan.

Taming Tiger Lohan

伏虎羅漢

Pindola

Precious ring with magical powers,
Infinitely resourceful.
Vigorous and powerful,
Subduing a ferocious tiger.

Pindola was a Brahmin and a general. Because he was devoted to Buddhism, which forbids killing, he was ordered by the king to become a monk. He joined a monastery in the mountains where he could hear a tiger howling every day. He said that the tiger was probably hungry and should be fed some vegetarian food; otherwise, the tiger might become a man-eater. So, Pindola collected food from the monks and put it in a bucket which he left outside the monastery. The tiger did come for the food every night. After a while, the tiger was tamed, and Pindola was thus referred to as the Taming Tiger Lohan.

About the Translator

Stuart Alve Olson, longtime protégé of Master T.T. Liang (1900–2002), is a teacher, translator, and writer on Daoist philosophy, health, and internal arts. Since his early twenties, he has studied and practiced Daoism and Chinese Buddhism. As of 2015, Stuart has published more than twenty books, many of which now appear in several foreign-language editions.

Biography

On Christmas Day, 1979, Stuart took Triple Refuge with Chan Master Hsuan Hua, receiving the disciple name Kuo Ao. In 1981, he participated in the meditation sessions and sutra lectures given by Dainin Katagiri Roshi at the Minnesota Center for Zen Meditation. In late 1981, he began living with Master Liang, studying Taijiquan, Daoism, Praying Mantis kung fu, and Chinese language under his tutelage.

In the spring of 1982 through 1984, Stuart undertook a two-year Buddhist bowing pilgrimage, "Nine Steps, One Bow." Traveling along state and county roads during the spring, summer, and autumn months, starting from the Minnesota Zen Meditation Center in Minneapolis and ending at the border of Nebraska. During the winter months he stayed at Liang's home and bowed in his garage.

After Stuart's pilgrimage, he returned to Liang's home to continue studying with him. He and Master Liang then started traveling throughout the United States teaching Taijiquan to numerous groups, and continued to do so for nearly a decade.

In 1986, Stuart published his first four books on Taijiquan— *Wind Sweeps Away the Plum Blossoms, Cultivating the Ch'i, T'ai Chi Sword, Sabre & Staff,* and *Imagination Becomes Reality.*

In 1987, Stuart made his first of several trips to China, Taiwan, and Hong Kong. On subsequent trips, he studied massage in Taipei and taught Taijiquan in Taiwan and Hong Kong.

In 1989, he and Master Liang moved to Los Angeles, where Stuart studied Chinese language and continued his Taijiquan studies.

In early 1992, Stuart made his first trip to Indonesia, where he was able to briefly study with the kung-fu and healing master Oei Kung Wei. He also taught Taijiquan there to many large groups.

In 1993, he organized the Institute of Internal Arts in St. Paul, Minnesota, and brought Master Liang back from California to teach there.

In 2005, Stuart was prominently featured in the British Taijiquan documentary *Embracing the Tiger.*

In 2006, he formed Valley Spirit Arts with his longtime student Patrick Gross in Phoenix, Arizona.

In 2010, he began teaching for the Sanctuary of Dao and writing for its blog and newsletter.

In 2012, Stuart received the IMOS Journal Reader's Choice Award for "Best Author on Qigong."

Daoism Books

- *The Immortal: True Accounts of the 250-Year-Old Man, Li Qingyun* by Yang Sen (Valley Spirit Arts, 2014).
- *Book of Sun and Moon (I Ching),* volumes I and II (Valley Spirit Arts, 2014).
- *Being Daoist: The Way of Drifting with the Current* (Valley Spirit Arts, 2014)
- *The Jade Emperor's Mind Seal Classic: The Taoist Guide to Health, Longevity, and Immortality* (Inner Traditions, 2003).
- *Tao of No Stress: Three Simple Paths* (Healing Arts Press, 2002).
- *Qigong Teachings of a Taoist Immortal: The Eight Essential Exercises of Master Li Ching-Yun* (Healing Arts Press, 2002).

  Forthcoming
  - *Clarity and Tranquility: A Daoist Guide on the Meditation Practice of Tranquil Sitting.*
  - *Refining the Elixir: The Internal Alchemy Teachings of Daoist Immortal Zhang Sanfeng* (Daoist Immortal Three Peaks Zhang Series).
  - *Seen and Unseen: A Daoist Guide for the Meditation Practice of Inner Contemplation.*
  - *The Yellow Emperor's Yin Convergence Scripture.*
  - *The Actions and Retribution Treatise.*

Taijiquan Books
Chen Kung Series
- *Tai Ji Qi: Fundamentals of Qigong, Meditation, and Internal Alchemy,* vol. 1 (Valley Spirit Arts, 2013).
- *Tai Ji Jin: Discourses on Intrinsic Energies for Mastery of Self-Defense Skills,* vol. 2 (Valley Spirit Arts, 2013).
- *Tai Ji Tui Shou: Mastering the Eight Styles and Four Skills of Sensing Hands,* vol. 4 (Valley Spirit Arts, 2014).
- *Tai Ji Bing Shu: Discourses on the Taijiquan Weapon Arts of Sword, Saber, and Staff,* vol. 6 (Valley Spirit Arts, 2014).

  Forthcoming Books in Chen Kung Series
  - *Tai Ji Quan: Practice and Applications of the 105-Posture Solo Form,* vol. 3.
  - *Tai Ji San Shou & Da Lu: Mastering the Two-Person Application Skills,* vol. 5.
  - *Tai Ji Wen: The Principles and Theories for Mastering Taijiquan,* vol. 7.
- *Tai Ji Quan Treatise: Attributed to the Song Dynasty Daoist Priest Zhang Sanfeng,* Daoist Immortal Three Peaks Zhang Series (Valley Spirit Arts, 2011).
- *Imagination Becomes Reality: 150-Posture Taijiquan of Master T.T. Liang* (Valley Spirit Arts, 2011).
- *The Wind Sweeps Away the Plum Blossoms: Yang Style Taijiquan Staff and Spear Techniques* (Valley Spirit Arts, 2011).
- *Steal My Art: The Life and Times of Tai Chi Master T.T. Liang* (North Atlantic Books, 2002).
- *T'ai Chi According to the I Ching—Embodying the Principles of the Book of Changes* (Healing Arts Press, 2002).
- *T'ai Chi for Kids: Move with the Animals,* illustrated by Gregory Crawford (Bear Cub Books, 2001).

Kung Fu Books

- *The Complete Guide to Northern Praying Mantis Kung Fu* (Blue Snake Books, 2010).

Check out Stuart's author page at Amazon:
www.amazon.com/author/stuartalveolson

About the Publisher

Valley Spirit Arts offers books and DVDs on Daoism, Taijiquan, and meditation practices primarily from author Stuart Alve Olson, longtime student of Master T.T. Liang and translator of many Daoist-related works.

Its website provides teachings on meditation and internal alchemy, taijiquan, qigong, and kung fu through workshops, private and group classes, and online courses and consulting.

For more information as well as updates on Stuart Alve Olson's upcoming projects and events, please visit: www.valleyspiritarts.com.

About the Sanctuary of Dao

Established in 2010, the Sanctuary of Dao is a nonprofit organization dedicated to the sharing of Daoist philosophy and practices through online resources, yearly meditation retreats, and community educational programs. The underlying mission of the Sanctuary of Dao is to bring greater health, longevity, and contentment to its members and everyone it serves.

Please visit www.sanctuaryofdao.org for more information about the organization and its programs.

19798753R00187

Made in the USA
San Bernardino, CA
13 March 2015